PR

LAST GANGSTER IN AUSTIN

A rookie district attorney. A wily, backslapping multi-millionaire bail bondsman. And one of the biggest criminal investigations in Austin history. Jesse Sublett's book is both a riveting crime story and a character-rich study of Austin, Texas. It's smartly c   llently researched.

—SKIP HOLLAND   hor of *The Midnight Assassin: The Hu   st Serial Killer*

Once again Jesse Subl   he Lone Star State's capital lives up to its m   stin weird. Enjoy this romp back in time to   onnie Earle ruled at the courthouse and F   he salvage business.

—KATHRYN CASEY   hor of *In Plain Sight: The Kaufma   r Murders*

Jesse Sublett is a first-rate writer and researcher. Once again, he dives deep, exposing the creeps and bottom feeders of Austin's criminal past to create an engrossing portrait of district attorney Ronnie Earle at the dawn of his long and legendary career. *Last Gangster in Austin* is a great read.

—W. K. KIP STRATTON, author of *The Wild Bunch: Sam Peckinpah, a Revolution in Hollywood, and the Making of a Legendary Film*

Also by Jesse Sublett

NONFICTION

*1960s Austin Gangsters: Organized Crime
That Rocked the Capital*

Never the Same Again: A Rock 'N' Roll Gothic

*Esther's Follies: The Laughs, the Gossip, and the Story
Behind Texas' Most Celebrated Comedy Troupe*

Armadillo World Headquarters: A Memoir,
with Eddie Wilson

*Broke, Not Broken: Homer Maxey's Texas
Bank War*, with Broadus Spivey

History of the Texas Turnpike Authority

FICTION

Rock Critic Murders

Tough Baby

Boiled in Concrete

Grave Digger Blues

LAST GANGSTER IN AUSTIN

FRANK SMITH, RONNIE EARLE, AND THE END OF A JUNKYARD MAFIA

JESSE SUBLETT

UNIVERSITY OF TEXAS PRESS 🐂 AUSTIN

Requests for permission to reproduce material
from this work should be sent to:
Permissions
University of Texas Press
P.O. Box 7819
Austin, TX 78713-7819
utpress.utexas.edu/rp-form

∞ The paper used in this book meets the minimum requirements of
○ ANSI/NISO Z39.48-1992 (R1997) (Permanence of Paper).

Names: Sublett, Jesse, author.
Title: Last gangster in Austin : Frank Smith, Ronnie Earle, and
the end of a junkyard mafia / Jesse Sublett.
Other titles: Jess and Betty Jo Hay series.
Description: First edition. | Austin : University of Texas Press,
[2022] | Series: Jess and Betty Jo Hay series | Includes
bibliographical references and index.
Identifiers: LCCN 2021047955 ISBN 978-1-4773-2585-8 (cloth)
ISBN 978-1-4773-2398-4 (paperback) | ISBN 978-1-4773-2399-1 (PDF)
ISBN 978-1-4773-2400-4 (ePub)

Subjects: LCSH: Smith, Frank (Bail Bondsman)—Trials, litigation, etc. |
Earle, Ronnie. | Smith, Frank (Bail Bondsman) | Gangsters—Texas—Austin—
Biography. | Public prosecutors—Texas—Austin—Biography. | Organized
crime—Texas—Austin—History—20th century. | Trials—Texas—
Austin— History—20th century.
Classification: LCC F394.A953 S83 2022 |
DDC 976.4/31063—dc23/eng/20211018
LC record available at https://lccn.loc.gov/2021047955

Cover and interior design by Amanda Weiss

doi:10.7560/325858

*This book is dedicated to my wife,
Lois, and my mother, Elizabeth.*

CONTENTS

Every society gets the kind of criminal it deserves.

—ALEXANDRE LACASSAGNE,
CRIMINOLOGIST (1843–1924)

You must be crazy coming in here to raise a posse.
Frank's got friends in this room. You ought to
know that.

—BARTENDER TO MARSHAL WILL KANE
IN *HIGH NOON* (1952)

What does seem to be eternal about the job is dealing with the expectations that our most visible constituencies have of prosecutors. The police expect us to validate their actions. Crime victims expect us to ease their pain. The media expects us to be perfect, like they would be if they just had subpoena power. I call it subpoenas envy.

—RONNIE EARLE, TRAVIS COUNTY DISTRICT
ATTORNEY (1977–2008)

LAST GANGSTER IN AUSTIN

AUTHOR'S NOTE

DEEP DIVE

In the early 2000s I started writing a memoir, published in 2004 by Boaz/Ten Speed, titled *Never the Same Again: A Rock 'n' Roll Gothic*. The highlights of my music career in Austin and Los Angeles, along with my gradual transition to being a writer, offer a lot of humor and absurdity. There's even some levity in my battle with Stage IV neck cancer, with less than 10 percent chance of survival. Woven through the narrative is the story of the murder of my girlfriend, Dianne Roberts, by a serial killer in August 1976 and the long trail of dire, life-challenging repercussions that follow such a thing.

A nineteen-year-old electrician named Lyle Richard Brummett confessed to the murder. He also confessed to killing a sixteen-year-old girl in Kerrville in 1975 while serving as an accomplice in the murder of an eighteen-year-old girl on the same occasion. The case was a big story in the media, with maddingly frequent updates, as if they feared I might somehow forget about the moment I came home from a gig and found her body. To retain some semblance of sanity, I would leave the room anytime the local news came on television. I read no daily newspapers at all that year.

When I started researching the case for my memoir, almost twenty-five years had gone by, but the time gap did nothing to ameliorate the pain of confronting unpleasant aspects of the story for the first time. It was hard work. I camped out at the courthouse archives in Travis and Kerr Counties, interviewed people, and spent hundreds of hours with newspaper microfilm. My focus was the period between August 1976, when the Austin murder occurred, and May 1977, when Brummett and his accomplice were shipped off to prison for their crimes.

During this research I kept running into stories about Frank Smith. On some days there would be a story about the Brummett case and a story about Frank Smith in the same section of the paper. At least once (February 5, 1977, for example), the stories were on the front page.[1] Who was Frank Smith? I wondered.

Smith, I learned, was a powerful man who had powerful friends. Convicted twice on car-theft charges, the second time for switching VIN numbers from salvaged autos to stolen ones, his criminal record and unsavory associations did no apparent harm to his wrecking yard business. He thrived on being quoted in the media, and reporters happily accommodated him. He was a six-foot-two, XXXL loose cannonball of contradictions: he would swagger and brag about how rich he was, then make a self-deprecating remark about being a modest country boy. The son of a Baptist preacher, he often quoted the Bible, even in response to a message that a murder-for-hire contract had been fulfilled.

At the same time, newly elected Travis County district attorney Ronnie Earle, already a potent political figure in Travis County, had taken the reins at the county prosecutor's office—the most powerful in the state, as its purview included felony crimes committed by state officials, corporations, and other large entities—and during his first month in office, indictments were secured against Frank Smith, setting the stage for one of the biggest criminal trials in Travis County history. Earle had entered public life as a municipal judge at the relatively young age of twenty-six, and he shone during his brief career as a state representative from Austin (1973–1976). As the new district attorney, however, Earle had everything to prove: plenty of rivals were betting on him to fail. The courthouse good old boys viewed him as an outsider. Candidates for district attorney were expected to ascend to the post via the usual ladder: that is, inside the county courthouse system, starting out as assistant district attorney or assistant county attorney. To the courthouse good old boys, Earle had nervily strutted over from the legislature, thrown his hat in the ring, and walked away with the prize.

But Earle showed them. He obtained a conviction in a difficult case, then set about reforming and reinventing the DA's office. In his thirty-two years as Travis County's district attorney, he proved to be not only passionate about the law but also a tireless, visionary reformer who kept looking for new ways to address social problems, always guided by the notion that his job was not just to put criminals in jail but to see that justice was done.

One thing I particularly admired about Earle was his commitment to the rights of victims of violent crime. Earle backed the efforts to strengthen and improve the victims' rights division of the Texas Department of Criminal Justice, which still notifies me each time Brummett is considered for parole. They make it easy to respond by letter or to personally speak to a member of the Texas Board of Pardons and Parole. I appreciate this function very much. A private organization, People Against Violent Crime (PAVC), also provides much-needed assistance. Verna Lee Carr, who was then PAVC's codirector, introduced me to the Victim Services Division, coached me on how to write a parole protest letter, and assisted me in various other ways.

As intrigued as I was by Frank Smith's story, it took me a while to get around to writing it. Ronnie Earle retired as district attorney in 2008. When I began this book in 2020, I spoke to his wife, Twila Hugley Earle, who informed me that he was in ill health. He died two weeks after my initial phone call. Twila told me that Ronnie had read my memoir and even made some margin notes in it. Some months later, Twila and I began talking off the record, and by midsummer we transitioned to interviews. These memorable sessions became essential to my project, and not just for the information she shared. With her fierce intelligence, she gave me more insight into what Ronnie Earle was like as both human being and authority figure than any other source.

Various people told me that Ike Rabb and his family were salt of the earth and that I would like them a lot. As it turned out, the family had doubts about reopening old wounds. Additionally, they were grieving the recent death of a family member. After a few weeks, however, I got the word: they were eager to cooperate. Denise Ormand, Ike's daughter, told me that reading my memoir convinced her that I was worthy of their trust. As a fellow victim of violent crime, she said, she had confidence that I could relate to their point of view. Two days after that conversation, Denise dropped off two boxes of invaluable news clippings, letters, a journal, and a valuable portion of the trial transcript—all of which greatly enhanced the project.

Another source of inspiration for this project was the quality of the reporting on Frank Smith's criminal career. In particular, the witty, lively (and often humorous) sentences in *Austin American-Statesman* reporter Bill Cryer's reporting seemed to jump off the page. Cryer was one of the first people I called, and once he agreed to participate, I felt confident that I could do a credible job on this book. Cryer's memory was good, his gift for witty repartee intact, and our interviews were something I looked forward to. He said to call anytime, that he would do whatever he could to help. After I sent him a brief progress report, he replied with a slyly cryptic text:

> Looks like you're in a deep dive. I hope you stay sane.
> I believed there was a Frank Smith virus and it was

contagious. When I remember those days now, decades later, I shudder. He will haunt you if you're not careful. Everything he touched turned dark.[2]

I thanked him for the warning, put a date on the quote, and got to work.

JUNKYARD OWNER SHOTGUNS ROBBER: WAS IT A SETUP?

December 3, 1976, fell on a Friday, the last month of the Bicentennial year, and the crack-crackle-boom racket just after sunset sounded a lot like fireworks. Except it wasn't. People were shooting at each other at the Austin Salvage Pool, a sprawling automotive boneyard out in the rural/industrial borderlands of southeast Austin. Inside the converted chicken coop that served as a temporary business office were the owners, Isaac "Ike" Rabb and his wife, Jane, plus two employees and a friend, five human beings in a small shed suddenly invaded by a man wearing a jumpsuit and a rubber monkey mask and brandishing a big silver 9-millimeter automatic. The blur of movement in the back of the room was Ike diving for a 20-gauge shotgun on a shelf four feet from where he stood. Pistol rounds flew this way and that, denting a steel file cabinet here, punching an adding machine over there, until Ike fired the double-barreled blast of number 4 duck shot that ended the argument. When the dust settled the near-sighted bandit lay dead in a pool of his own blood, his

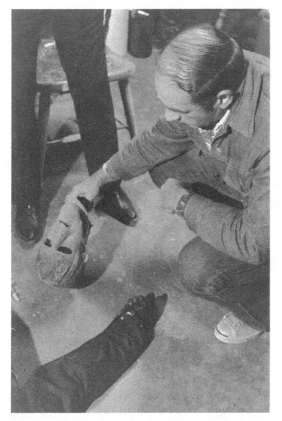

Sheriff Raymond Frank, squatting, his Converse sneakers showing, retrieves
the rubber monkey mask worn by gunman Willie McKnight (on the floor,
arm outstretched), who was killed during the attempted robbery of the
Austin Salvage Pool.

identity and his embarrassment concealed by the rubber mask
that fit so snugly he'd been forced to leave his eyeglasses in the
getaway car.

Someone said there were more bandits in the yard. Ike took
the dead robber's pistol outside and traded volleys with two
other masked men until they spun around and ran like hell in
different directions, leaving behind their car, a 1975 black-over-
yellow Ford LTD.

Back in the business office no one had a scratch. Ironically, when the robber had appeared an employee was on the phone with the sheriff's office, arranging for a deputy to escort Ike and Jane Rabb on the way to the bank for that day's deposit, which included an unusually large amount of cash, $15,700.

A salvage pool acts as a broker between insurance companies and salvage dealers, auctioning off the company clients' wrecked autos to dealers. For their efforts the Rabbs collected a modest fee of $25–$40 for each wreck they processed. At two dozen or so wrecks auctioned off every two weeks, it was a modest enterprise. In the last transaction that day, a salvage dealer named Frank Smith came and stuck around for two hours, haggling on prices and other details, and finally, at almost six p.m., he'd agreed to pay cash for "about 50" wrecked cars.[1] The biggest auto salvage dealer in the area, Smith was a multimillionaire bail bondsman who had been to the penitentiary twice, and over the past two years he had caused the Rabbs so much trouble and grief they'd reluctantly agreed to transact with him if he paid in cash. The total for the fifty wrecks that day came to $15,000. Smith handed over the money, signed the paperwork, got in his green Cadillac, and drove away. Witnesses spotted the Cadillac as it stopped alongside a yellow Ford LTD coming the opposite direction. Minutes later, the monkey-masked gunsel stepped into the office, demanded the money, and started shooting.

After the dust settled and the police sirens died out, fingers pointed to Frank Smith as the mastermind of the failed robbery plot. You might ask: Why would a man pay a broker $15,000 for some wrecked cars only to hire three hoodlums to come and steal it back? But that was exactly what Smith had done, according to investigators and the county grand jury. Later, federal arson charges added to Smith's troubles, and the FBI charged him with hiring a hit man to murder an important witness. It was one of the biggest criminal cases in the history of Travis County.

The opposite number to Frank Smith's black-hat picaresque was Ronald Dale Earle, the district attorney–elect of Travis County, who was universally known as Ronnie. Born in 1942 and raised on a ranch outside Fort Worth, Earle came to Austin on the cusp of the sixties and found his heart and mind in perfect synch with the place. An Eagle Scout, an intellectual, and a wanderer in the woods, Ronnie graduated from the University of Texas, campaigned for equal rights, went through law school, and headed for places where he might fulfil his potential for greatness. He was appointed municipal judge in 1969 at age twenty-six, the youngest judge in the state. In 1973 he resigned to run for state representative, won election, and was serving his second term in 1976 when he set his sights on the district attorney's office. In that election he outpolled his two rivals in the spring primary and was sworn in on January 3, 1977. The first item on his agenda would be prosecuting Frank Smith.

No one was calling Austin the "Live Music Capital of the World" in the 1970s, and yet a post-1960s, progressive, music-oriented culture had already taken root in the city. Much of the miniboom in musical activity could be credited to a music hall and arts emporium called the Armadillo World Headquarters, which was situated just south of downtown in a structure originally built to serve as a military armory (a dream that was, fortunately, mostly unrealized).[2] Black Austinite musicians and entrepreneurs east of the Interstate 35 divide had already laid the groundwork for an Austin blues scene at venues like the Victory Grill and Ernie's Chicken Shack, setting the stage for clubs like Antone's, the One Knite, and Soap Creek Saloon, where the tradition became the popular cultural currency of the city.[3] The city's politics were no less progressive than the music scene, reflecting the early seventies tidal wave of victories by liberal Democrats. Austin had a long-haired (though balding) former student activist named Jeff Friedman as mayor, and a mop-topped district attorney named Ronnie Earle. Although his hairstyle probably helped make him seem like a kindred spirit to Austin musicians and other luminaries, it was Earle's aura of openness, agile intelligence, and strong visionary streak that sealed the deal.

In practice, Ronnie Earle sought to shift the focus of the district attorney's office to helping underserved communities rather than merely throwing their populations in jail. Earle imagineered a new identity for the offices under his purview. He led the creation and adoption of innovative programs to assist victims of crime, child abuse, and spousal abuse. He committed resources to the underlying causes of crime and to community justice. Much more than a simple law-and-order man, Earle was an innovator, a seeker, a visionary. He passionately strove to create new ways to promote justice within the community, to forge meaningful partnerships between citizens, neighborhoods, and government.

Despite being the champion of many ideals and political positions that are typically characterized as "liberal," Ronnie Earle was no coddler of criminals, and he came down on Frank Smith like a ton of bricks, using every weapon at his disposal.

By December 1977 Frank Smith had been a fixture in the headlines for years, one reason being highly publicized accusations of corruption and impropriety involving his bail bond business. Many of the specifics of the complaints about Smith also involved Travis County sheriff Raymond Frank. A retired Air Force veteran, Raymond Frank had run for county sheriff in 1972 on a platform that included promises to modernize the sheriff's department and to stop harassing pot smokers. Appearing in Converse sneakers and eschewing cowboy hats, Frank came on, superficially at least, like a breath of fresh air. He won election in 1972 and was elected again four years later, with a slogan—"The sheriff who shoots straight"—implying that he was honest and incorruptible. But to his many detractors his scraggly comb-over implied just how fraudulent he was.

Isaac "Ike" Rabb and his wife Jane at the sheriff's office after the December 1976 robbery. Ike and Jane were a perfect match: he was soft-spoken and easygoing, while she was hyperactive, operatic, and effusive.

Only two weeks prior to the robbery, *Statesman* reporter Bill Cryer had listened to Ike and Jane Rabb relate incidents of intimidation and harassment they'd suffered at the hands of Frank Smith, behavior that reeked of Mafia-style tactics. Sheriff Frank had ignored the Rabbs' complaints. Cryer had qualms about publishing the story, however. He told his editor, Ray Mariotti, that it seemed primarily "a dispute between two business rivals."

Cryer was already home for the day when the robbery occurred. A phone call from city editor Mariotti sent him charging into action like a dog with a bone in his teeth. Cryer drove out to the crime scene and spoke with detectives, the Rabbs, and others, then returned to the *Statesman*'s downtown headquarters and called Frank Smith. Sometime later that night, Cryer hammered out a classic piece of city crime reporting for the December 4, 1976, morning edition. The story appeared on the front page above the fold, with dramatic photos and a headline that posed a mysterious question: "Junkyard Owner Shotguns Robber: Was It a Setup?"

> A robber who apparently knew that $15,000 had just been delivered to an auto salvage yard east of Austin was shotgunned to death Friday afternoon in an exchange of gunfire with the owner of the firm. The robber and his two companions had just missed the man who delivered the money, Frank H. Smith, a prominent Austin bail bondsman and auto salvage dealer. The dead man's two accomplices were still at large Saturday.

To any reader who is paying close attention, the three short sentences of Cryer's lead were exploding suitcases of weird possibilities. The inner structure of the piece was a crime-story-within-a-crime-story, the outer structure was all context: the previously reported stories on the grand jury investigations into sexual abuse, arson, and corruption in high places, and implications that these were only the tip of the fatburg.[4] Later in the piece Cryer deftly quoted Smith, letting Smith flip the story over, making himself the intended victim, not the Rabbs. "Something stinks about this," Smith said. "I was set up out there. My underworld sources tell me that I was very, very fortunate to have gotten away."

There were fine reporters besides Cryer who followed the case and wrote well about it, but Cryer's reporting always stood out for its precision, clarity, and wit. Looking back today, Cryer is modest when complimented about his work, and one gets the feeling that after all these years, he is still a bit amazed that the things he so eruditely described actually occurred.

Ronnie Earle, the hero of this story, took on hundreds of other important cases in the decades following the Frank Smith trial. He became famous for prosecuting corrupt politicians like US Congressman Tom DeLay, a Republican, and Democratic politicians, too, though he was more passionately invested in social justice and helping to "reweave the fabric of community."

Yet in 2007, when a reporter asked Earle about his perspective on his long and eventful career, he replied that his finest moment was the first big case he tried after taking office, *The State of Texas v. Frank Smith*.[5]

BAPTIST PREACHER'S SON

I never saw a religious bone in Frank's body. I'm
a very serious Presbyterian, but I'm a secular
Presbyterian and I just don't talk about religion,
and I never would have thought about religion
with Frank.

—CAROL FOWLER

Frank Smith was big. Big as in larger than life. He stood six-
foot-two, midsection like a beer keg, arms and legs like tree
trunks. He drove a big Cadillac. He wore a big, 10.5-karat diamond ring. Big impression. Big as in big business: in 1956, when
he was twenty-six, he founded what was to become a used auto
parts empire in Central Texas, armed with $16 in his pocket and
a cashier's check for $6,000, the latter the proceeds from the
sale of his maternal grandparents' farm, which he invested in a
ten-acre wrecking yard on Interstate 35 just a few miles north of
the Austin city limits.[1] By the 1960s Frank Smith & Sons Auto
Parts was the biggest wrecking yard in Austin, and Frank Smith
was a power to be reckoned with.

In 1974 Smith applied for a license to write bail bonds and
rented an office in the Stokes Building, located practically across
the street from the Travis County Courthouse. Bail bondsmen

Sunday church services with Frank and Dorothy Smith and two of their three offspring. Letisha sits between her parents; Marlo (*to Dorothy's left*) was the youngest. Although Frank's father was a Baptist preacher, the son was largely ambivalent about organized religion.

were not supposed to promote their services inside the sheriff's office or the jail, but it wasn't hard to find their business cards and even the occasional office calendar advertising their services. And then there was Frank Smith, the super promoter, the walking billboard, who tried to make sure that potential customers encountered him on the way in. "Frank Smith kind of took up residence on the bench outside the sheriff's office," said John Sutton, former reporter for the *Statesman*. "So, he'd go, 'Well, if you need a bondsman, I can take care of you.'"[2] The Travis County sheriff at the time was retired Air Force officer Raymond Frank. We'll learn more about him later.

Frank Smith & Sons Bail Bonds soon achieved a monopoly in the bail bond trade in the county, raking in up to a million dollars a year from that pursuit alone. Controversy swirled around Smith's approval for a bail bond license: he was still on federal parole when he applied for it. He had been released in 1971 after serving twenty months on a felony conviction for running an interstate car-theft ring. He also had two prior felony convictions.

Down on East Eleventh Street strip in East Austin, the pimps and prostitutes and other nocturnal hustlers recognized Smith's green 1975 model Cadillac and mountainous silhouette. Prostitutes and dealers called his name, shook his hand, and reveled in his cornpone jive. Pimps and drug dealers identified with his accoutrements: the Cadillac, the chunky gold rings, the leather jacket, the two-tone shoes, the woman on his arm who was not his wife nor his color. As a bail bondsman, he had worked this community of crime, vice, and alternative lifestyles like a preacher doling out personalized blessings for every member of his flock. Frank was a necessary hero/villain of the underground economy, a Robin Hood who came on like Fat Elvis, the Junkyard Elvis, the redneck rapper, the godfather of mixed metaphors, Don Corleone as reimagined for *Hee Haw*.

Bail bonds meant power. Earning 15 percent on each bail (a nonrefundable fee), Smith made money hand over fist. *Statesman* reporter Bill Cryer had witnessed Smith's influence over the day-to-day destiny of his bailees, particularly the many repeat offenders in his clutches. Cryer intuited that it would be easier for the average newspaper reader to comprehend the situation by stating it in economic terms, calculating that Smith's 15 percent fee on all the bail bonds he had written in Travis County between July 1974 and December 31, 1976, would have totaled $979,416; the amount of bonds that Smith wrote in other counties (Hayes, Harris, Burnet, and McClellan, to name a few) is not known. The potential profit, however, apparently motivated Smith to invest his time and money cultivating friendly relationships with the respective sheriffs in those jurisdictions.[3]

Equally significant, he accumulated a vast roster of regular customers and strange allies, a pool of social misfits perpetually indebted. They worked cheap. Some ran errands; others hunted down bail jumpers. At various times Frank would hire a team of misfits to burn down a house or a business, possibly even a church. Frank strung them along. Homeless losers found a seat at the Smith family dinner table. But if he signed your bond and you failed to check in or pissed him off, he might go off (withdraw) your bail and let you ponder your errors in a cell at the county jail.

In the early 1970s, when Doyne Bailey was a homicide detective with the Austin Police Department, he bumped into Frank regularly on his second-shift patrols on the east side.[4] As a seasoned detective as well as a Baptist youth minister, Bailey was a keen observer of human behavior. His first encounter with Smith, he said, was a revelation: "Frank was trolling the prostitutes, the pimps, you know, those folks, on East Eleventh Street," Bailey said. "I stopped him and asked him for his driver's license, and he just took over the stop, he just chatted about everything. He told me all about his business. He was just very talkative, very friendly [*laughs*]. I was just taken with how charming he was."

In 1967 Bill Cryer was a city reporter covering the federal courts for the *Statesman*, and Smith was a prominent salvage dealer on trial for interstate car-theft conspiracy. Tall, long-limbed, and handsome, Cryer looked like the kind of person you might sit next to at a bar and tell your troubles to. He was and is still a good listener, too. "Frank came up to me and we chatted for about thirty minutes before I realized who he was," said Cryer. "Then, years later, he shows up again as the biggest bail bondsman in Travis County. Frank was a character, a strange man, and I wouldn't put it past him to do anything he desired to do. He was completely amoral."

Frank Hughey Smith was born in Waco, Texas, on March 10, 1930. The stock market had already collapsed, prompting the economic and social disaster known as the Great Depression.

By the time young Frank took his first steps, the unemployment rate was 25 percent. He learned to read just in time to spell D-U-S-T, as in Dust Bowl, the midsection of the country being peeled away by Armageddon-like storms.[5] On December 7, 1941, three months shy of his eleventh birthday, Japan bombed Pearl Harbor, prompting the United States to enter World War II. From these chronological beats, one might almost wonder if Smith's birth was a bad omen for civilization.

His father, Rev. Roy L. Smith, was a Baptist preacher, well-known in Waco and other parts of the state, where he conducted revival meetings that frequently took him away from his family and flock at Brook Avenue Baptist Church in Waco, where he served as pastor from 1936 to 1964. Family members knew Reverend Smith as strict and stern, a hard taskmaster. Frank would name his first daughter after his mother, the former Letisha Hughey. "He loved and adored his mother," said Letisha Taylor. "He was crazy about her."[6]

Smith appears to have been hard-working and industrious as a youth, "boarding and breaking horses at the age of twelve," according to Taylor, though he still had energy left over to entertain a mischievous, rebellious streak. "My dad got in trouble a lot," Taylor said. "He wasn't a bad kid, but he was always in trouble." Reverend Smith "would beat the hell out of Frank, but that's just what they did back then."

"I don't know if my dad's life would've turned out differently, but they were just never allowed to have anything," she said. "One time a relative bought him some new shoes, and my grand-dad made him give them back. His dad said a Baptist preacher's kid don't deserve new shoes."

Frank was notorious for pulling practical jokes. A donkey on the third floor of West Junior High? No one was surprised when they learned the identity of the donkey wrangler. Frank's prankster side attained the quality of lore as such incidents were retold and perpetuated by his contemporaries.

One such contemporary was W. S. Foster, former state legislator, former judge, and publisher of a biweekly paper called the *Waco Citizen*. Over the course of at least two decades, Frank Smith figured regularly in Foster's column, "Observations," often introduced to readers as "My friend Frank Smith."

Frank's burro prank made Foster's column numerous times, often in conjunction with reporting on criminal matters that were perhaps not as amusing. Foster wrote on February 4, 1977, for example, that "as a youngster in Waco, he was always pulling some prank, such as putting a burro on third floor of West Junior High, [or] stealing Judge D. W. Bartlett's gavel in the 54th district court." Smith happened to be present in Judge Bartlett's courtroom because he was on trial "as the master-mind in (the) theft of a Baptist preacher's auto."[7]

"When he was a kid, my dad started hanging out at the Dodson wrecking yard," said Taylor. Dodson Auto Salvage in Waco is where Frank Smith got the idea to go into the salvage business. "He saw the money they were making," Taylor said. Young Smith also saw that the salvage business attracted people who were involved with organized crime, an association that did not dampen his enthusiasm for the enterprise. Some of these people would be doing business with Frank in later years.

Frank Smith made tentative moves to follow in his father's footsteps, salvaging souls instead of wrecked cars. He enrolled at Baylor University. The precise date is uncertain, the duration short.

Frank became a father on March 4, 1946, at age fifteen. He and his wife Jaimie named the child Frank Hughey Smith Jr.[8] The birth notice in the *Waco Tribune Herald* identified the mother only as "Mrs. Frank Smith," but she wasn't Frank's Mrs. for long.

"She walked off and left him," said Taylor. "She just couldn't handle children." Fortunately, Frank Senior's aunt, Sallie Mae Hughey, willingly served as a surrogate mother to help raise the child. Frank, Sallie Mae, and Frank Junior moved to a family farm outside Waco. "Sallie Mae was always in my dad's life," added Taylor.

Letisha Smith, wife of Rev. Roy Smith, mother to Frank and his sister Miriam, was hospitalized for a minor procedure on August 16, 1950. She died at 9:50 p.m. that night.[9] Her death had been caused by a hospital error during a blood transfusion, but that part was not mentioned, Taylor added.

Twenty-six years before he was accused of hiring gunmen to rob the Austin Salvage Pool, Frank Smith was convicted and sentenced to prison in connection with a series of armed robberies in the Waco area. Investigators learned that Smith was the person who cased the locations, coordinated the heists, and fenced the booty.

Although not much is known about 1949 case, facts relating to his role in a series of robberies between late 1950 and 1951 were thoughtfully provided by his accomplices. The initial accounts were related by a trio of thieves who confessed to a residential robbery in Waco, a home-invasion robbery in the town of Marlin, and the armed robbery of the bar at the Hotel Corsicana in Corsicana. When arrested on January 28, 1951, two of the young men were driving a car that had been specifically stolen for use in another robbery. Two other accomplices had stolen the car, they said, on orders from Frank Smith, who told them that "he needed a car for a robbery, that he needed it in a hurry; and that he would pay us $100 the next day." In the statement given by one of the car thieves, we find serious questions regarding Smith's honesty and esprit de corps, which echo those of Smith's criminal accomplices in 1976.

> The next day I read in the paper where Harris and Hunt [who did the actual armed robberies] got caught by Officer Sam Day in the Mercury. I saw Frank later on and he said that he didn't see how Harris and Hunt could get so

dumb. He never has paid us the $100 for stealing the car for him.[10]

If Frank Smith, twenty-two-year-old convict, didn't already have political connections, he must have developed them during his first term in Huntsville, partly through the influence of his father. In any event, Frank's network of helpful acquaintances included Gov. Allan Shivers, Texas's first three-term governor. Shivers was a hardcore segregationist and populist demagogue, his too-long tenure in office marked by a hard-right turn and an epidemic of corruption (including the Veterans Land Board case and an explosion of insurance companies being looted by their executives, with the help of corrupt politicians).[11]

Shivers's last term in office coincided with Frank Smith's first term in prison. As governor, Shivers had final approval on all decisions made by the Board of Pardons and Paroles. On January 6, 1956, he approved the early release of Frank Hughey Smith. A full pardon, signed by Shivers's successor, Price Daniel, was issued October 22, 1957.[12]

Smith was paroled to Austin. According to the release plan, instead of aiding and abetting car thieves, Frank Smith would be working as a chauffeur driving a state official. The official, if singular, could have been Governor Shivers himself.

The three-term governor, along with the head of the state prison system, Dr. George John Beto, must have seen a bright future for the twenty-seven-year-old twice-convicted felon.

Letisha Taylor said she remembers visiting Allan Shivers with her father at the old Pease Mansion, where Shivers resided after he left office. She believes her father was assigned to be the governor's chauffeur. "My brother, Allan Beto Smith, was named after Gov. Allan Shivers and Dr. George John Beto," said Taylor. Beto was appointed to the TDC (Texas Department of Corrections, later changed to Texas Department of Criminal Justice) board by Shivers in 1953, right around the time Frank entered prison, so we could say that Smith and Beto served those three years together. From 1962–1972, Beto served as both director of TDC and chief of chaplains.

"Dr. Beto and my dad were very close," said Taylor. "He helped us get into St. Paul Lutheran school. When Beto died, my dad was torn up about it. He served as an honorary pallbearer at the funeral."

Political consultant Nick Kralj, who was acquainted with Dr. Beto as well as Frank Smith, admired the former but not the latter. "Frank was affable," said Kralj, recalling their encounters in the early 1970s when Kralj operated a popular downtown eating and drinking establishment called the Forum. The place attracted customers from a varied cross section of society but was particularly popular with the sporting set. Kralj kept his distance from Smith, he said, after learning from a former inmate at Huntsville that Smith had been a "building tender" during his incarceration there. "Building tenders did the dirty work for the guards," Kralj explained. "They were the enforcers. They were brutal."[13]

Indeed, Beto's failure to end the Texas prison system's use of building tenders remains a dark stain on his record.[14]

Years later *Statesman* reporter Bill Cryer was shown evidence of the friendship between the former convict and the prison director. "I was in Frank Smith's house one time, and it was loaded down with old clocks," Cryer said. "I was admiring them and he said, 'Yeah, this old grandfather clock was given to me by the warden at Huntsville.' I said, 'The warden at Huntsville gave you a clock?' He said, 'Yeah, he's a good friend of mine.'"

Somewhere in that same collection—perhaps Cryer's host failed to point it out—was a vintage clock given to Smith by Gov. Allan Shivers.

W. S. Foster announced Frank's release on February 23, 1956, in his newspaper, the *Waco Citizen*. Foster wasn't a bit surprised that his friend had regained his freedom in such a short time. In a later column Foster remarked that Smith "has always been a close friend to most state politicians. Governor Allan Shivers enabled him to get released from the Texas penitentiary . . . to chauffeur a state car."[15]

Frank Smith was still on parole between January 1956 and the fall of 1957, a period of almost two years. In an interview with Bill Cryer in December 1976, Smith said that his first job after getting out of prison was working for a contractor for a dollar an hour.[16] During his second year in Austin, he borrowed money from his aunt, Sallie Mae Hughey, to found Frank Smith Auto Parts. In what must have seemed an unusual partnership at the time, Rudolph Robinson, an African American mechanic, worked with Smith from the very beginning. By all accounts, Robinson was instrumental in the success of the new venture. Letisha Taylor said that the number of people her father trusted implicitly could be counted on one hand, and Rudolph Robinson was one of them: "No one else in knew more about Frank than Rudolph."

Unfortunately, Robinson is now deceased. Attempts to locate family members and friends in 2020 were unsuccessful.

THE EAGLE SCOUT

> Ronnie liked to read Westerns, like Zane Grey
> novels, and I remember when they were going
> into a meeting with Ronnie they would say they
> were going "riding with the Purple Sage." An
> other thing they would say is, "We're going into
> the bog . . ." Because if you got into a meeting
> with Ronnie, you couldn't get out.
> **—MARNIE PARKER**

During his first decade or so in public service, Ronnie Earle wore
his dark brown hair long, styled in what would pass as a Beatles
haircut. The members of the famed Liverpool quartet, however,
had better teeth. Two of Earle's front incisors fought for space in
his mouth, and one was noticeably chipped. Around the courthouse, Earle's unruly ivories combined with his sense of ethics
to inspire a saying: "The only thing crooked about Ronnie Earle
is his teeth."

Ronnie Earle's hairstyle was something he shared in common
with the new generation of lawyers and judges who were getting
their start in public service and government in the mid-to-late
sixties, many of whom tended to be left-leaning in their political

Ronnie Earle, speechifying during the 1976 election for district attorney.

views. Carol Fowler came to know Earle first as a political reporter and later as an investigator in his Public Integrity Unit.
With her razor wit, fierce intelligence, and broad streak of icon-
oclasm, Fowler and Earle must have gotten along well. A habit
of always speaking her mind, which endeared her to many, was
not quite as welcome in her hometown of Amarillo, where it got
her fired from the *Amarillo Globe-Times*.[1]

"I gave a negative review of John Wayne's *Alamo*, and I was
terminated for that," she said.[2] "I was also listed in the paper as
a proto-communist," she said, "and that was not funny in 1958."

Fowler suffered no fools regarding John Wayne's Texas jingo-
istic fantasy, but when asked about Ronnie Earle and what made
him tick, she slowed down and spoke in almost Biblical cadences.
"A lot of people, I think, had trouble understanding just how
serious Ronnie Earle was about justice, just because he laughed

a lot and he was easy to know and friendly and open," she said, "but Ronnie was very, very serious about justice."

Fowler mentioned a case in which a young African American man had been murdered during the term of Earle's predecessor, Bob O. Smith. Because there had been no trial, the parents of the murdered boy kept coming in to see Earle after Smith left office. "The police were pretty sure who had killed this young man but they couldn't make a case," said Fowler. "His parents used to visit Ronnie all the time, wanting to see if he could do something. Ronnie would say, 'They were here, they want justice, and there's no such thing for them.'" The fact weighed heavily on Earle, she said. "I had a lot of respect for Ronnie."

Ronald Dale Earle was born February 23, 1942, in Fort Worth, Texas, and raised on a family cattle ranch north of the city near the town of Birdville. Whenever he discussed the ideals that shaped his outlook on life and his work as a public servant, Earle always credited his family and the place he came from. His parents, Lowleta Muse Earle and Charles C. Earle, both came from large families. Charles worked for General Dynamics for forty years in order to hold on to the ranch, a sheep-feeding station founded by Ronnie's great-grandfather in 1850.

"I always had a bunch of aunts and uncles around, and they were important people in our lives," Earle said in an interview with the *Austin Chronicle*'s Michael King and Jordan Smith in 2008. "If you got too far out of line, there was an old uncle or aunt who grabbed you by the collar and set you straight."

The point of the story, Earle would tell you, was that "the most progressive and innovative things" he worked to achieve in life were informed by his family environment. "It really informs . . . most of the things I've tried to do as district attorney, especially the most progressive and innovative things that we have done in this office," he said in the same interview. "And the reason is because the law doesn't teach you how to act. . . . What I have come to call the 'ethics infrastructure' teaches you how to act. And that is in that work of mommas and daddies and aunts and uncles and teachers and preachers and neighbors and cousins and friends—that's where you learn how to act, not from the law."[3]

The early phases of Earle's development—Eagle Scout, lifeguard, student council president—lend a sense of logic and inevitability to his professional career and commitments as political activist and reformist public servant. Interestingly, for a person who chose a life of public service at a young age, he craved time alone.

"Ronnie had a sister that was much younger, but for a long time he was the only child in the family," said Twila Hugley Earle, his wife. "He spent a lot of time out in the pastures, roaming around by himself. He really liked to be outside."[4]

The late Jan Reid, a journalist and author from Wichita Falls, knew Earle for several decades. Jan wrote that whenever their paths crossed, their conversations ranged "from high school football—he played linebacker for the Birdville Buffaloes, who were in my high school's district (Wichita Falls)—to Cynthia Ann Parker," the subject of a popular captive narrative from Texas's frontier days that reveals more about the hysterical paranoia regarding Euro-American miscegenation than it does about the culture and tradition of indigenous Americans.[5]

"Ronnie's nose cartilage was rearranged in sparring bouts with football teammates that were orchestrated by his coaches, and his fingers are gnarled from playing tackle and linebacker; his right ring finger wags loosely on his hand," Reid wrote in a profile of Earle published in *Texas Monthly* in 2005. "He told me he played his last game for the Birdville Buffaloes—against storied rival Wichita Falls—with a broken ankle: 'I went to that game on crutches and came home on crutches. They beat us fifty to nothing.'"[6]

Earle remembered Birdville as a tough little hamlet, a good place to get in a brawl over a simple disagreement or by simply looking askance at a hot-tempered knucklehead. Birdville, which had a population of four hundred in the midfifties, was on the northern outskirts of Fort Worth, a city with such an active and violent underworld it was called "Little Chicago" when Earle was growing up.[7]

"The mob tried to move into Fort Worth in the fifties," Earle said, "but they were run out because (local crime) was too well-organized. That was a legend that I assume was true, because there were gangland murders all over the place when I was growing up."[8]

Earle's gangland memories could have been related to incidents during the bloody reign of "Cowboy" Benny Binion, a former rumrunner and horse trader who gained complete dominance over illegal gambling in Dallas between 1936 and 1946—and he controlled a good portion of the same in Fort Worth, too. Murders of both the premeditated and incidental kind were also a fact of life on Fort Worth's Jacksboro Highway, a pipeline of prurient delights that offered big-name music stars, gambling, and prostitution, a seven-mile stretch of forbidden recreation where any fewer than two ambulance calls was a slow night.

Closer to home, there was Haltom City, a wide spot in the road between Birdville and Fort Worth proper that was home to 5,700 residents in 1950 and, according to newspaper reports from the time, an impressive number of corrupt cops and gangsters. Earle must have felt a sense of déjà vu when, sixteen years after leaving Birdville for Austin, he was sworn in as district attorney of Travis County and the first major criminal indictment to land on his desk was *Texas v. Frank Smith*, a case with a supporting cast of police characters from Haltom City. In December 1976 the first gunsel who came through the door of the Austin Salvage Pool office and started blasting with his pistol was Robert Willie McKnight, a Haltom City used car dealer and burglar. Two other men charged in the case, an ex-cop and another used car dealer, were also Haltom City bad boys.

At numerous junctures in his early life, Ronnie Earle might have bumped into some of these same Haltom City toughs, because at various times he considered becoming a cop, a writer, and a college football player. The idea of becoming a lawyer did not appeal to him because the only attorneys he'd seen in person were the ones who loitered at the local courthouse looking like "vagrants."

Everything changed after he drove down to Austin and enrolled at the University of Texas in the fall of 1960. Austin, founded as the capitol of the Republic of Texas in 1839, was 121 years old; Earle was nineteen. In the coming decade, as major cultural shifts and political upheaval regularly jolted the country, Austin would begin making waves of its own. A sense of destiny must have been in the air. "I thought I'd come to heaven; I really did," Earle said. "To be here with people who could have an argument without having a fistfight, and I thought that was really remarkable—that you could actually do that. And who thought different things. And I saw people with beards and things."[9]

The youth-quake of the post–World War II era was just beginning to remake the country's political, social, and cultural norms—and Austin, with its large population of university students, was about to emerge as an important force in the national progressive movement. Earle found kindred spirits here who helped him find his voice.

As of 1960 Austin boasted a new reservoir in the middle of town called Town Lake, just waiting to be discovered between its weedy, trash-and-junk-littered banks. The beautification programs led by Lady Bird Johnson to make the lake more attractive and accessible would come later.[10] There were also abundant natural swimming holes, of which the premiere was Barton Springs, a place many considered sacred, in addition to being somewhere to have a howling good time. The courthouse crowd, campus activists, state legislators, lobbyists, and other political operators gathered at local watering holes like Scholz Garten, Threadgill's, and the Tavern, eating, drinking, and breathing politics. Austin was a company town and the company was politics. Austin was, after all, the state capital and home of the premiere state university, and it was also the headquarters of the (Lyndon B.) Johnson political machine and Johnson media empire. During LBJ's combined twenty-two years in the US House and Senate, he made certain that his home constituency benefitted from federal spending. As of January 1961, LBJ was vice president under John F. Kennedy, and Kennedy seemed so youthful, energetic, and smart that the future seemed full of promise and possibilities.

To be young, filled with physical and intellectual energy, living and working in a place that vibrates with a sense of vitality, self-importance, and destiny, can be extraordinarily affirmative and inspiring. Austin in the 1960s to 1970s was like that, a kind of mecca for intellectuals and artists of all stripes, a good place for someone like Ronnie Earle to realize his potential.

TEXAS PACKAGE

Well, you know, most of these outlaws are real likeable people. Like Frank Smith, I really liked him. As a matter of fact, I liked him as much as my brother. He was just interesting. He was a fascinating person, and one of these people you'd sit down and talk with and it was amazing the things that would come up in conversation. But it seems like to be a gangster you have to have a real good personality. That's my theory anyway.

—DOTTIE ROSS

In 1960 Frank Smith shifted some of his great energies toward raising a family. A few years earlier, a friend named Charlie Krueger had introduced him to Dorothy Lee Eixman, a subject of Krueger's affections who would soon become the love of Frank's life. "Charlie was so sweet on my mom," said Frank's daughter, Letisha Taylor. "She was in the hospital and my dad went along with him to visit her. That's when he met my mom."

Frank was still on probation when he and Dorothy starting dating, and she was still legally married to someone else when

Letisha was born in 1960. According to Letisha, the divorce was finalized and Dorothy and Frank were married within two years or so. A brother, Allan Beto, was born in 1963, joined by a sister, Marlo Lee, in 1970.

Dorothy Lee Eixman grew up in Cameron, a town located seventy-two miles northeast of Austin. Her father ran a joint there that offered alcoholic libations and the services of prostitutes. Reporter Bill Cryer got to know Dorothy during Frank's series of legal entanglements in the midseventies. "She would bend my ears for hours about her childhood growing up in a whorehouse. She would tell me all about how during World War II she would sneak down and watch the soldiers having sex with prostitutes." The tone of the friendship changed from day to day, sometimes by the hour. "She would call me up and cuss me out all the time about things I had written about Frank," Cryer said, "and then the next day, she'd meet me down at some cafe and regale me with stories about her checkered past." In lengthy personal conversations with Cryer's wife, Dorothy would share personal advice. Keep "a happy home," she said once, "and your husband will never leave. He might run around with other women, but he will always come back home."

Among all the partisans of Frank Smith, none was as zealous or devoted as Dorothy. "She had the look of a hard woman," Cryer wrote in the *Statesman*. "Her flint-sharp features and piercing eyes were those of a strong will. She was partisan, fiercely loyal and accustomed to battle."[1]

At the time Cryer wrote those words, the harsh, flinty look he described was also due to Dorothy's near-fatal battle with brain cancer. From a distance, however, what you noticed first was her slender, petite figure and long, straight hair under a scarf or floppy beret. She had the dark, exotic look of a sixties rock star's girlfriend. Photos of Frank and Dorothy together not only speak volumes about their love for each other but also convey the sense that they occupied an outpost that smoldered from their you-and-me-against-the-world mindset.

"My mom was beautiful," said Letisha Taylor. "She was a semi-nude calendar girl. I saw them a couple of times." The photographs were "tasteful," she said, "like Victoria's Secret today." Her father told her that Dorothy "always regretted" having posed for the photos and was fearful that the photos would someday come back to haunt her.

In contrast to her super extroverted, late-night-trolling husband, Dorothy Smith was an intensely private person. She preferred staying at home, keeping a beautiful home, and supporting Frank in whatever capacity he needed.

Affectionate indulgence for children and pets alike was a constant in the Smith household. "My dad loved animals," said Letisha Taylor. "We had all kinds, but he loved his cats." Frank even bought a pair of Bengal tigers, but their tenure was short-lived. "My mom put her foot down," said Taylor. "We always had horses. He brought our horses home to have colts in our neighborhood house." On the lonely days when Frank was out and the Smiths were burdened with problems, a pet parrot named Molly was always there for Dorothy, lending companionship and comic relief. One of Molly's frequent exclamations was, "Fuck Frank! Fuck you, Frank!"[2]

Dorothy "Dottie" Ross, who lived four houses down from the Smiths on St. John's Road, couldn't help but notice the happy aspect of the Smith family. "Our daughters started first grade together," she said. "I met Frank's wife Dorothy when she and I would go out to the street to meet the kids when they got home from school." Dorothy Ross was known to friends as Dottie, but Dorothy Smith also answered to that name. To make matters more confusing, at the time Dottie Ross's last name was Harding. Her husband, George Wayne Harding, was also known as George Harper.

"My little girl and her daughter, Letisha, and her brother Allan, played together a lot," said Ross. "Frank just adored my daughter, and in fact he wanted to adopt her. One day I happened to look down the street, and he had a little Ford Falcon and all three kids were in the car and they had a pony in the back seat. The horse had his head out the window, and the kids were so excited. He was always doing crazy things like that. He was always real good to the kids. He would take them out to where his aunt lived on the farm and entertain them."[3]

"There's a lot of garbage out there about Daddy," Letisha Taylor said during a phone interview. "A lot of the garbage is true, but I adored my dad. Frank was definitely a colorful character. Believe me when I say my dad had way more good than bad. When someone's house burned down, or someone lost a child, he took money or food the very next day. When someone lost their job, my dad offered help right away. My mom took over groceries. Daddy paid people's medical bills, utility bills, put countless doctors and attorneys through college. . . . Our table always had a homeless person or two that my dad gave odd jobs to and supported. . . . He let homeless folks live in the old warehouse at the wrecking yard."

By the late 1960s the Smith family resided at 11402 Hunters Lane in North Austin, a short four-mile drive to the salvage yard. The home was a substantial two-story brick structure with notions of a country estate, set back from the street and bordered by a brick wall. The spacious home had ample room for entertaining Frank's friends and associates from low and high places, and space to display his growing antique clock collection.

Tressa Granger was Letisha's best friend from her teenage years, and they remain close today. Tressa's father, Ned Granger, was the county attorney from 1968–1976. Ned Granger grew up in China Spring, a rural, unincorporated community twelve miles from Waco. A classmate, Dave Richards, remembered Granger being "as country as anybody ever was." "He wore overalls to school every day," said Richards, "and I'm sure he was the first member of his family to get out of high school."[4] Granger went to college at A&M, then worked for a year or so before deciding that he wanted to be a lawyer. He went to law school at UT, passed the bar, and in 1964 got a job as assistant district attorney. In 1968 he campaigned and won election to county attorney, one of the most powerful offices in the county except for district attorney.

Letisha and Tressa began driving at an early age. "I was driving myself to school at fourteen," said Letisha, "and at fifteen, driving Sam Johnson [brother of Lyndon Johnson] around was my job." As Frank's designated driver for various friends and cronies, Letisha said she drove Sam Johnson to appointments with both doctors and bartenders, and at various other times she helmed her daddy's Cadillac for Bob Bullock (then state comptroller, later lieutenant governor), Ann Richards (state treasurer, later governor), and other important figures.

Likewise, in her early teens, Tressa Granger proudly served as her father's designated driver; the cargo of influential personages riding in Ned's Plymouth Duster was virtually interchangeable with Letisha's.

An impressive number of police characters—a term used by law enforcement to identify ex-convicts, prostitutes, pimps, burglars, and other "known criminals"—worked in the local auto trade as mechanics or used car salesmen. Some of them simply carried a business card identifying themselves as used car salesmen. Timmy Overton, titular leader of the Overton Gang, actually did operate a small used car lot adjacent to the transmission shop he co-owned with his father on East First Street, but the car lot was a front, and, as FBI agents put it, the shop became a "crime school." During their heyday in the 1960s, Timmy Overton and his crews were suspected of burglarizing more than twenty-four small-town banks across Texas and the Southwest.

A safe burglar or pimp might claim to be a used car salesman as a hedge against being charged with vagrancy, a catch-all ordinance used against suspected criminals when no proof of criminal activity was available. Collecting expensive automobiles was also a means of parking illicitly gained funds for quick conversion when cash was urgently needed. Local characters, including the Overtons, also kept a couple of autos in reserve or traded them with cohorts as a means of creating confusion among the cops who kept them under surveillance.

By 1966 Frank and Dorothy were the proud parents of two small children: Allan, three years old, and Letisha, six and starting first grade. To neighbors like Dottie Ross, the Smith home must have seemed a little like Camelot, a "happy home," as Letisha described it, with horses to ride at Aunt Sallie's farm, lots of pets and toys and love in the house. Business at the wrecking yard was booming.

"He made a lot of money," said Dottie Ross. Recycled auto parts were much more commonly utilized in those days, she said. "He had one of the biggest wrecking yards there was. . . . It was a big, big deal and he had lots and lots of cars, and he would just hold onto them, because he had ten acres there. He had a car-crushers, too, so if he wanted to raise a bunch of money quickly, all he had to do was crush all those cars that were stripped already and he'd have a big wad of money."

Smith's salvage business made a considerable amount of money, but apparently the legitimate side of the operation wasn't enough to satisfy him. On Thursday, April 27, 1967, warrants were served by agents from multiple law enforcement agencies, including the FBI, sheriff's department, APD, and the Texas Department of Public Safety (DPS). One individual was also arrested in Las Vegas, Nevada. In Austin arrests were made on St. Elmo Road in South Austin, in far North Austin at Frank Smith Auto Parts, and at other addresses. Frank Smith and nine other individuals were taken into custody. The ten had been charged with participating in "a conspiracy to steal late model cars, switch serial numbers and license plates from wrecked vehicles of the same model and transport the stolen cars to Nevada and California to sell."[5]

Among the ten defendants was Richard Hinton, a thirty-two-year-old used car salesman with a well-documented heroin habit. Hinton was part of the constellation of shady characters around Frank Smith that included Timmy Overton and his syndicate of bank burglars, pimps, and gamblers. Hinton pleaded guilty to the car-theft conspiracy charge and agreed to testify against his fellow coconspirators.

Bail was set at $10,000 for the other defendants. At arraignment all nine pleaded not guilty. Frank Smith was the only one who made bail that day. Surety for his bond was signed by Hattie Valdes, Austin's most popular bordello madam, and a major Austin real estate developer named R. C. Wilson.

Dottie Ross explained the basic methodology of the car-theft operation. "They would use the VIN number from the salvaged car," she said. "They'd buy a wrecked car, and get a title for it, and find a good one, and trade numbers on it." A stolen car plus a matching wrecked car with title was known in the trade as a "Texas package."

By Monday, September 12, 1967, the first day of testimony, four conspirators had changed their pleas to guilty, leaving Frank Smith and four other defendants on trial.[6]

The trial lasted five days. The jury heard testimony from coconspirator James Alfred Boyd, who said he'd gotten involved in the scheme with Frank Smith back in the fall of 1965. Boyd recalled that Smith had said, "Jimmy, if you use your head, we'll make $100,000 apiece . . . and get out of this thing quick."

When Smith took the stand, he denied everything. He had not, he said, furnished the car ring with titles, license plates, or serial numbers from wrecked cars on his lot. He did, however, purchase several wrecked cars that were involved in the government testimony, but he knew nothing about how the titles and serial numbers came to be switched to stolen cars. He often sold wrecked cars to people and conveyed the titles to them, but he had never sold just a title and serial number, nor did he know anything about what became of the cars and titles after he sold them, he said.[7]

After the prosecution rested, defense attorneys sought to undercut the government's case by smearing the state's witnesses. As a notorious heroin addict who was also serving as a government witness in several other cases (including two burglary cases that involved one of the Overton brothers as well as a fellow car-theft coconspirator), Hinton was an easy target. The other four defendants who'd cut deals with the state were fair game, too.[8]

The jury deliberated for a day and a half before returning a verdict of guilty for all five men. The heaviest sentence was imposed on defendant Michael Gurleski, who had done the actual stealing of autos on request: he received two concurrent five-year sentences plus a three-year sentence to run consecutively. Frank Smith got two five-year sentences to run concurrently.

While his fellow conspirators began their prison terms, Frank Smith remained free on bond as his attorney, Bob Looney, worked on appeals. On January 29, 1969, Frank's father, Rev. Roy L. Smith, was being taken to a hospital in Waco when his heart beat its last.[9] After the burial in Waco, the *Waco Citizen* reported on February 9, with an ironic choice of wording, "His son, Frank Smith, and family, were here from Austin where he is a prominent business man in wrecked car trafficking."

The fight to overturn the verdict of the 1967 district court went all the way to the State Supreme Court, where Looney's plea for a new trial was denied. On August 12, 1969, Frank Smith, thirty-nine years old, was removed to Leavenworth to begin his sentence. By that time, Gurleski was already free on parole.

THE BIG HASSLE

Early on, some kids at school would make fun of
me because I might come to school with grease
under my fingernails and they'd call me "grease
monkey" or "junkyard dog," but after the robbery
people seemed to think that the Rabbs were a rich
family [*laughs*], and I didn't get any of that junk
yard dog or grease monkey treatment anymore,
it was, *Oh y'all are better than everybody . . .*
—GEOFF RABB

Summer vacation 1969: as soon as the school year was out in
the Bellaire suburb of Houston, Texas, Isaac "Ike" Rabb and his
wife, Jane, and their children picked up and moved to Austin.
One of Ike's associates in the insurance business had hired him
to take over the management of a fledgling new business called
the Austin Salvage Pool. The operation, which bore a surface
resemblance to the average auto junkyard, was a brokerage that
contracted with insurance companies to sell their wrecked autos
to salvage buyers through regular auctions.

"A salvage pool was a rather new idea in the insurance business, because it tried to take the sale of the salvage away from the adjusters," Ike Rabb explained. The idea was to keep everyone "a little more honest," he said, but "that was very much bucked by the salvage buyers and the other people who were in it, because it removed a direct contact for them."[1]

The honesty issue, Ike explained, involved salvage dealers paying kickbacks to adjusters, along with other corrupt practices. Part of the resistance to the salvage pool business model described by Rabb was from Frank Smith, then the biggest salvage dealer in the region. Smith passed along word that he would make sure that the Austin Salvage Pool failed. Fortunately for the Rabbs, however, during their first six months in Austin, Smith was preoccupied with his legal problems, and by the end of 1969 he was back in the penitentiary.

In the months that followed, Ike and Jane Rabb heard terrible stories about Smith from people who had dealt with him. Although nothing came of Smith's threats during the time he was in jail, the Rabbs came to realize that the salvage business in Austin was something that Smith regarded as his private fiefdom. For all the troubling stories they heard about Smith, the months that followed passed peacefully.

In the early years, as they struggled to establish the business, the Rabbs were just barely getting by. In the beginning the operation might take in a dozen cars a week and hold an auction every two weeks. With a brokerage fee of only $25 per car, the income was meager enough to make them wonder if moving to Austin had been a bad idea. "I took the whole family there," said Ike. "It was not what I expected it to be, because most of the people in the business didn't like us. It was a brand-new world."

Ike Rabb is an educated, erudite, soft-spoken man with a New Orleans accent that has been only slightly tamed in the years since he moved from his native New Orleans. The seemingly unlikely prospect of Rabb serving as the implacable obstacle in the way of Frank Smith's schemes is made more understandable by reading the ten-page diary in which Rabb recorded key incidents from his troubles with Smith. Rabb's wry, understated wit is on every page. "Neither of us [Rabb and his wife Jane] had ever heard of Frank Smith," he wrote about their initial arrival in Austin. "This was soon corrected since Automobile Dealers throughout the area quickly brought us up to date on the doings of the local celebrity member of their fraternity."[2]

Jane Rabb was Ike's opposite in many respects: talkative and vivacious, a keen business operator, and fierce guardian of the family. By all reports Jane held the family and the business together during the most trying periods of the 1970s. It was Jane who collected and maintained a vast trove of newspaper clippings, photos, and other materials documenting their encounters with Frank Smith and his eventual downfall. The materials fill seven large scrapbooks.

Ike and Jane brought their five children to Austin: two boys, Geoff, eight, and Jonathan, seven; and three girls, Ann Marie, sixteen, Denise, ten, and Reneé, two.[3]

Ann Marie had lost her hearing after a bout with measles and high fever when she was less than a year old. The State School for the Deaf in Austin made the family relocation more attractive. "It was like, 'Well, we can do this,'" said Ann Marie's sister Denise. "So we moved to Austin and started to grind out a living here."[4]

Born in 1931, Ike was a product of both city life and farming country, New Orleans and Slidell, Louisiana. Drafted during the Korean conflict, he was spared from combat at the last minute. As Geoff Rabb told it, "Dad was on the boat at the dock leaving for Korea when they said, 'We need somebody for admin work, can anybody here use a typewriter?' He raised his hand and they pulled him off the boat."[5]

Ike Rabb attended Loyola University in New Orleans and married the former Jane Maurice Griffin, of Birmingham,

Alabama. Ike was working for an insurance company in New Orleans, writing bonds for contractors, when a sales position in Houston beckoned. With some reluctance, he and Jane decided to make the move. Ike said that he was "very sad to leave New Orleans," and that in Houston the new job "didn't pan out." "But then I had a friend, Ron Yeates, who started the first salvage pool in Houston." Yeates talked it up, urging Ike to take the opportunity to operate the new salvage pool he had just opened in Austin.

The business's original manager hadn't worked out, Rabb said. "He was homesick. He didn't like Austin. He wanted to get back to Houston." The Rabbs moved to Austin, took over the operation, and a year later arranged a large loan from Jane's family so they could purchase the business from Yeates. "We became owners rather than employees," Ike wrote in the account of the Rabbs' war with Frank Smith. "The concern for the business became thus more personal and direct."[6]

"Dad was driving the wrecker and Mom managed the office," said Denise, remembering their first years in Austin. "From my recollection, it was always pretty much hard work."

The Rabbs' family residence was on the premises of the salvage yard. All the siblings grew up with the business, and they all helped out. Geoff, who turned eight the year the family moved to Austin, remembers being a first-grader in the Bellaire suburb of Houston, "playing spin the bottle ... doing mischievous stuff, running around with older kids ... then one day helping load the trailer to move to Austin."

"My earliest memories are that every day we'd have chores to do," said Geoff. "We had guard dogs, and my job was to feed them and clean out their pens." Fifty years later, he can still reel off their names: Ranger, Bullet, and Queenie. Ranger was not much of a guard dog, he said, but Bullet was mean.

Denise, who turned eleven in 1970, said, "We lived at the business, and I didn't want anybody coming over because we lived with all these wrecked cars." A beat later, she added, "Actually, it was quite interesting. We played around with the cars and the motorcycles, and we got in trouble a lot, doing things we weren't supposed to do with the cars."

Frank Smith was released on parole in April 1971, after serving twenty months and fourteen days. Smith paid his first visit to Austin Salvage Pool sometime that summer. "Jane and I first met him then when he walked in on us announcing what he would do if I would not let him use the pool," Ike wrote in his diary. "This consisted principally of promising to sue us and each and every company we do business with for discrimination as outlined by the Civil Rights Act. He said he was not going to allow us to stand in his way. The tone of this statement was intended to convey (and did) physical threat. This meeting disturbed me a great deal."

Rabb stood his ground but offered that he would poll his insurance company clients to see if they approved or objected to Smith's participation in the Salvage Pool. Rabb was "shocked" by the answers he got from his clients. "Strangely enough," Ike wrote, "none of the people I called had any objection to Mr. Smith's bidding on their cars, which was a puzzling turnabout from past statements." The 180-degree change in attitude was, he added, "the beginning of a long series of anxieties and frustrations."[7]

Trouble with Smith began immediately after the August 1971 auction. Smith refused to abide by the established purchasing protocol: instead of paying Austin Salvage Pool for the purchase price plus their fees, he made out checks to the insurance company. It was, as Rabb describes it, "not a large item but a troublesome one."

Smith pestered their insurance company contacts with various complaints about ASP, taking up their time with long, contentious rants in which he would "slur and demean our operation," wrote Rabb. Finally, in the interest of bringing peace to themselves as well as their clients, Ike and Jane agreed to go along with Smith's wishes. But the troubles continued. Smith kept finding new ways to hassle them and make their lives difficult. In each conflict, the actual point of contention was often minor, but whenever the Rabbs refused to make a special accommodation, Smith blew it up into a full-blown confrontation.

"First, he has some objections to some facet of our operation," Ike wrote. "Then he tells us how he wants to do it. Objections are raised . . . [and] long, wasteful phone conversations begin. . . . Smith threatens legal action against us, our customers, and God knows who else, and gets in as many digs as he can about us with our customers."

Smith even treated the Salvage Pool's closing time as means of igniting conflict. "Mr. Smith always seemed to arrive 15 to 30 minutes before closing time and carry us past the time set to shut the doors in order to serve him," Ike wrote.

Smith began insisting that new titles be exchanged at the point of purchase. Normally, there was a lag time of several weeks before a new title cleared the Department of Motor Vehicles. The standard procedure in purchasing a vehicle was for the buyer to consummate the sale, take possession of the car, and wait for the new title to arrive in the mail. But Frank Smith refused to pay for the cars he purchased at auction until he had the new title in hand. Smith always bought a large number of wrecks at each auction—often upwards of 90 percent. The yard at ASP began stacking up with his cars. When the titles were ready, Smith would show up just before or after closing time, knowing that it would take hours to move all the vehicles, causing more arguments and confrontations, plus more barrages of phone calls to the insurance companies and other salvage dealers, voicing complaints, slander, and outrage regarding his nemesis, the Austin Salvage Pool.

Every time Ike and Jane relented, acquiesced, or went out of their way to accommodate Smith, he found other ways to annoy and harass them. "The business was ours," Ike wrote. "It had prospered a little, but we had really worked hard for the progress and Smith seemed to be a threat to it at all times." Even more than the prospect of losing the business, they worried about Smith's reputation for violence, for being "ruthless and half crazy." "Certainly, my contacts with him had done nothing to dispel the paranoid theorem," he wrote. "We were scared and it was agonizing."

Smith harangued Ike and Jane over their payment procedures, refusing to submit a single check to them that covered both the seller (the insurance company) and the brokerage fees (Austin Salvage Pool). He also refused to pay the two-dollar fee on envelope drafts. After much haggling, Ike wrote, Smith agreed on the former but never capitulated on the latter.

The feud continued. Once again, Ike and Jane decided that since they couldn't get rid of Frank Smith, they "might as well find ways to get along with the bastard," and that is where things stood at the beginning of 1976.[8] At that time, no incidents of violence had yet occurred, not even a fist thrown in anger.

BEST JOB HE EVER HAD

When Ronnie Earle was appointed municipal judge by the Austin City Council in 1969, much was made of the fact that at age twenty-six, he was the youngest judge in the state, the youngest ever appointed in Austin. Ronnie was the wunderkind, and that vibe stuck with him for the rest of his professional career.

After graduating law school, Earle became involved in politics and the engine of state government. He landed a job as a state budget examiner under Democratic governor John Connally, an important ally of Lyndon Johnson who had served as secretary of the Navy under John Kennedy and was governor of Texas 1963–1969.[1] Earle met Connally for the first time in 1966 when he came to the Governor's Mansion to interview Connally for the *Daily Texan*. Connally was impressed with a paper Earle had written in law school titled "The Fire This Time: Urban Riots and Ghetto Violence."

Later, Earle worked as a legal assistant under Connally, but he still found time to lead an effort in Austin to end housing discrimination on the basis of race, in the first campaign of its type in the city. Earle was a busy young man, driven by a combination of vision and ambition. During this hectic time he married Barbara Ann Leach Earle. They had two children, Elisabeth Ashlea Earle and Charles Jason Earle.

During Earle's two terms on the municipal bench, he was a pioneer in the use of personal bonds. Releasing a defendant on a personal bond meant taking their word that they would show up for their day in court. If they didn't, they would owe the county the full amount of their bail. The very low percentage of no-shows was a powerful argument for the eventual extinction of bail bondsmen.

A cash bail bond was the amount set by a magistrate to guarantee that the accused would show up for court. Unless the individual was able to post the proscribed amount in cash in escrow with the court or, alternatively, to post unencumbered property worth twice the amount, the individual would be incarcerated until the trial date. Attorneys could and did write bonds, but usually for their own clients.

There was one more alternative: paying a bondsman a fee, usually 15 percent of the full amount of the bail. The fee was nonrefundable. If the bailee failed to show up in court, the bondsman would forfeit the full amount of bail. Bailees who failed to appear were known as bond jumpers. The people who were hired to track them down were known as skiptracers and bounty hunters.

If a person was hard put to scrape together 15 percent of the bail amount, finding cash to hire a lawyer was probably out of the question. The system was unduly hard on the indigent and the downtrodden and a magnet for corruption. Some judges used bail as a punishment, as if being charged with an offense meant guilty as charged.

Earle became an advocate for statewide reform of bail bond laws and proposed a personal bond system across the state. "We have people spending weeks and months in jail awaiting trial simply because they don't have the money to pay to get out," he told a reporter in 1975. "And I'm not talking about those who are given higher than usual bail when a judge considers them too dangerous to walk the streets or too likely to skip town."[2]

Earle called it "a sham and a disgrace . . . Machiavellian and medieval . . . probably the only part of the justice system that has never been touched by any intelligent approach." By contrast, release on a personal bond could be accomplished after the court was able to ascertain that the individual had a certain degree of stability and reliability in the community. The qualification process was not unlike a credit check or job interview.

At the end of his two terms on the bench, Earle estimated that he had released between six thousand and ten thousand people on personal bond, including people charged with "serious misdemeanors and felonies, people charged with everything from driving while intoxicated to armed robbery and even murder." Many were indigents, he pointed out, and yet only 2 percent of them had failed to show up in court.

Bobby Earl Smith, a young attorney in the 1970s, hailed the personal bond office as a turning point in county history. "The reason we have a great personal bond system today," he said, "is that we had such abject corruption in the bail bond system before. The bail bonds business was dirty, dirty, dirty. The bail bondsmen gave money to all these political candidates, . . . and it was a corrupt, self-perpetuating system."[3]

Travis County's personal bond program started out on a shoestring during the so-called Summer of Love of 1967. Originally, the program was a project run by students at the University of Texas Law School. Staffed by law students working for free, over a six-month period the program helped persons who would have otherwise been paying professional bondsmen a total of $22,000 for their release from jail.[4] The estimated annual cost for running the program was $16,000.

Two years after the county took over the program, it was still underfunded and without a real office.[5] The two counselors who vetted defendants operated out of a cramped area in the middle of the hall on the third floor, the only consolation being that the probation counseling office was in a very similar space. It's an ill wind that blows no good, however, and the critical overcrowding at the old courthouse helped draw more attention to the need for expanded physical infrastructure as well as passage of bail reform and personal bond programs—not only in Travis County but across the state. Ronnie Earle would be at the forefront of that movement, too, first as a member of the legislature, later as Travis County district attorney.

Earle liked to refer to his judgeship as "the best job I ever had," but during his second year on the bench, he found himself on thin ice with the mayor and members of the city council. At a seminar on drug abuse in Dallas, Earle replied to a question from a state senator about marijuana, stating that "to consider marijuana a narcotic is absurd."[6]

Mayor Roy Butler, a wealthy car dealer (honored in *Time* magazine in 1972 as the top "Quality Car Dealer" in the country) hit the roof when he heard about Earle's drug remark. In a Trumpian breach of protocol, Butler blasted Earle in the press for criticizing the state's drug laws, ignoring the scientific basis for the statement: marijuana is not a narcotic. Period.

Three district judges voiced their support for Earle's right to exercise free speech. Earle said he was "shaken" by the criticism, especially since it was made in public at a city council meeting. After some consultation with his advisors, along with Earle himself, Butler decided to cool it and the kerfuffle died out.

In 1972 the *Austin American-Statesman* raved that "Ronald Earle must be the best-known municipal judge Austin ever had." Texas Supreme Court justice Thomas M. Reavley called Earle "one of the outstanding young judges in the state."[7]

In August Earle announced that he was resigning as municipal judge to accept the position of chief counsel for the Texas Judicial Council. The council, the official agency that monitored performance of all state courts, was also charged with making recommendations to the legislature for improvement. A prestigious position, the job suited Earle's ideals as well as his ambitions.[8] During his time on the council, Earle developed recommendations that helped make the Texas court system easier for citizens to access and understand. Barely nine months had gone by before he saw an opening for getting his judicial reforms made into law.

A special election to fill the Texas House seat vacated by representative Don Cavness (who was running for an open senate seat) was set for July 17, 1973. Earle resigned his position during the first week in June, and when making his announcement for the house race, he left no ambiguity about his rationale for running.

In a speech before the West Austin Democrats, Earle said, "I'm very concerned about laws and how they affect people." The following January the state legislature would be holding a convention for the purpose of writing a new state constitution. It was Earle's intention to be the head of the committee charged with writing the judicial article of the new constitution. "This convention gives us the opportunity to provide this state with a people-oriented constitution."[9]

In the July 17 election, Earle won handily, polling three times as many votes as either of his two opponents. In October 1973 Earle distinguished himself by being the first publicly elected official to call for the resignation of Richard Nixon after Nixon fired special prosecutor Archibald Cox during the Watergate investigation. The firing scandal would be remembered as the Saturday Night Massacre. Nixon was forced to resign in disgrace the following year.[10]

During Earle's first term in the house, he helped bring justice to hundreds of persons convicted as felons for possession of small amounts of marijuana under the state's previously draconian drug laws.[11] The previous legislature had reduced the penalty to a minor misdemeanor but had failed to make the law retroactive. At Earle's request, Gov. Dolph Briscoe appointed him head of Project STAR (Social Transition and Readjustment), which granted pardons to inmates, helped them find employment, and assisted their transition back into society. In an interview with the *Austin Chronicle*, Earle stated that he had received a certificate from the labor department recognizing the program as the most successful ex-offender rehabilitation program in the United States.

In January 1974, one year short of a century after the state constitutional convention of 1875, which had produced the extant state constitution, the sixty-third legislature convened as a bicameral constitutional convention. Earle achieved his goal of chairing the judicial committee and authored the judicial article for the new constitution. Unfortunately, the convention lost its momentum due to partisan bickering over certain issues, particularly the right-to-work provision, which was strongly opposed by labor groups. As the convention dragged on, the upcoming May primary "also served as a political distraction for many legislators campaigning for reelection," according to the entry in the Handbook of Texas Online article on the constitutional convention of 1974.[12] The convention closed on July 30, 1974, three votes shy of approving a document to submit to voters.

In the fall general election Earle steamrolled his Republican opponent, Max Jackson, polling 76 percent of the vote to win a second term.[13] Prison reform and public employee rights were among his top priorities. In his work on behalf of the Austin–Travis County Transportation Study Committee, Earle sought more participation from communities and neighborhoods in partnership with government agencies. The study would later serve as a model for Earle's social justice projects, in which participation by communities affected by crime and violence (along with law enforcement, the courts, and even the perpetrators of crime and violence) participated in the planning of criminal justice reform. As ever, Earle wanted government to be more responsive, more accessible, to the people it served.

THE TWO FRANKS

He was a very interesting man. He obviously was
powerful in those days, and he was, let's put it
this way, he was well-fed and wore a lot of jewelry.
We certainly weren't friends but we got along.
He would talk to me and spend some time with
me. Sometimes, or all the time, I guess, I was a
little nervous when he would take me out for a
ride, but you know, he was the king in that
county and in that courthouse.

—RON LITTLEPAGE, ON FRANK SMITH

Raymond Frank was a man of many contradictions. As a candidate for sheriff in 1972, the forty-seven-year-old deputy clerk ran as a reformer. He had retired from the Air Force with the rank of lieutenant commander and boasted experience with the Air Force's OSI (Office of Special Investigations), although most of his working experience in intelligence appears to have been in the military prison system. His main opponent in the race, Sheriff Truett Ozias "T. O." Lang, carried a lot of baggage after twenty years in office, including the deplorable conditions in the

county jail and a nasty scandal over the secret electronic eaves-
dropping system installed in the jail in the early 1960s. Age was
an issue, too: Lang was sixty-two years old but he looked older.
He looked out of sync with the 1970s.

Raymond Frank came on like a breath of fresh air. He was fit,
an energetic jogger and talker. He wore tennis shoes to work.
His motto was "The Sheriff That Shoots Straight." His campaign was an aspect of the liberal makeover of the city, county,
and state legislature of the early 1970s, a movement that gained
momentum with the extension of voting rights to eighteen-year-
olds in 1971. By 1973 Austin even had a former campus activist
for mayor, Jeff Friedman. An effective and visionary admin-
istrator with a passion for equality and justice, plus an unruly
mustache and gregarious manner, Friedman was affectionately
known as Austin's "Hippie Mayor."[1]

During the campaign, Raymond Frank hit Lang hard with the
jail issue, inefficiencies, and certain improprieties, like the "Vote
for T. O. Lang" sign in the window of the sheriff's office. Frank
also vowed that under his administration, his officers would not
be busting or harassing people for possession of small amounts
of recreational drugs such as marijuana and psychedelics for personal use. Another plus for the youth vote was his "Let them
do their thing" policing of skinny-dippers at Hippie Hollow, a
popular clothing-optional swimming hole on Lake Travis. No
wonder Frank earned the support of people like Eddie Wilson,
founder of Armadillo World Headquarters, the South Austin
music emporium and counterculture incubator that helped establish Austin as a mecca for great music, art, and an enviable
lifestyle.

At the opposite end of the social spectrum from the Armadillo was the Alamo Hotel, a faded establishment on West Sixth
Street that was a hangout for old-school politicos, lawyers, and
questionable characters. Austin's top brothel keeper, Hattie

Valdes, enjoyed holding court there. So did Frank Smith. Sam Houston Johnson, the younger brother of Lyndon Johnson and a veteran political advisor, leased a four-room suite for office space and as a second residence. (Johnson also owned a home in Johnson City, where he and Lyndon had grown up.) Raymond Frank met with Johnson there to seek advice during his campaign. Political insiders and reporters generally assumed that Johnson was Frank's main political advisor and Frank Smith his chief financial backer.

People who were close to Smith, including daughter Letisha Taylor and longtime office assistant Dottie Ross, said that Smith not only funded but directed numerous political campaigns, particularly ones that would benefit his bail bond business. He was involved in campaigns for county sheriff in several other counties, including Hayes, Burnet, and McClelland.

Raymond Frank defeated T. O. Lang in the June primary election and took office at the beginning of January 1973. Frank followed through on his promises of tolerance for recreational drug users and skinny dippers, but on matters of integrity, his behavior was a source of disappointment, consternation, and bewilderment. He purchased fancy pistols for himself and friends by raiding the jail commissary fund, which was supposed to be for stationery and other items for jail inmates. He took lady friends along on expense-paid trips out of town to track hot-check writers and other scofflaws. The most persistent and serious of the improprieties and off-beat actions that occurred during Frank's administration, however, seemed to have Frank Smith as a common variable, and the first of such issues to emerge was Frank's blatant favoritism toward Smith's bail bond business.

Sheriff Frank approved Frank Smith's application for a license to write bail bonds in Travis County in March 1974, while Smith was still on federal parole on the 1967 car-theft conspiracy conviction. Smith's parole would not end until August 1974.

Frank Smith happened to enter the bail bond business at a time when the governor, the legislature, and the public were primed for reform of the bail system in the state. On June 16, 1973, Governor Briscoe signed SB 383, legislation drafted in response to highly publicized corruption scandals in the bail business.[2] Under the new law, every county with a population over fifty thousand was charged with creating a bail bond board that would coordinate with the county sheriff to establish local standards, collect fees, and issue licenses.

Each bondsman approved by the newly established Travis County Bail Bond Board was required to post either $5,000 cash or certified deposit with the county, or double that amount in property. Implementation of the new regulations hit a few snags early on. Certain bondsmen who had done the lion's share of the bail bond writing in previous years found themselves ineligible to do business in Travis County because of technicalities in their applications. Richard Hodges and T. W. Kincheon, both long-time bondsmen in Travis County, complained that they were being "shut out" of writing bails. Defense attorneys were also in an uproar after Sheriff Frank insisted that they, too, apply for licenses, pay the annual fee, and deposit surety with the county equal to twice the amount of bonds they wrote.[3]

Two of the most prominent defense attorneys in Austin, Roy Q. Minton and Charles B. Burton, announced that they were suing the sheriff over the new provision. Their firm, Jones, Blakeslee, Minton, Burton & Fitzgerald, Inc. (commonly known as Minton, Burton), wielded enormous power in Travis County.[4]

Sheriff Frank hired an outside attorney (Waggoner Carr, the former state attorney general) to defend his case. During the interim, as the case bounced around in court for the next two years, Frank exempted attorneys from the new rule. Frank Smith lent vocal support for the sheriff, saying that lawyers writing bonds for their clients was "very much a conflict of interest."[5]

When Smith started writing bonds, he placed a $5,000 surety deposit with the county. Within two years he had increased the amount to $125,000, which allowed him to write up to $1.25 million in bonds. According to some estimates, he was soon writing six out of every seven bail bonds in Travis County. By spring of 1975 the Junkyard Elvis had been crowned "the kingpin" of bail bonds by the press. "I do ninety percent of them, or so they say," he told writer Russ Million of the *Texas Sun*.[6]

On November 5, 1974, the district attorney of Tarrant County wrote a letter to the state attorney general asking for a clarification of Texas bail bond law, specifically asking if a bail bond board could refuse to issue a license to an applicant convicted of two felonies twenty years ago.[7] The question appeared to refer to an individual with a criminal record very similar to that of Frank Smith. Hill's reply, which cited precedent suggesting that the felonies were "too remote . . . to be admissible evidence on a character issue," also seemed to give considerable leeway to the local bail bond board to decide the issue based on its own investigation into the applicant's character traits: specifically, "honesty, truthfulness, fair dealing, and competency."

According to a state publication called the *Bail Bond Handbook*: "A person is not eligible for a license if the person has committed and has been finally convicted of a misdemeanor involving moral turpitude or a felony after August 27, 1973." Frank Smith had slipped in the gate by a margin of four years.[8]

Frank Smith & Sons Bail Bonds operated out of an office in the Stokes Building at 314 W. Eleventh Street, next to the Travis County Courthouse. Office stationery had the motto "Let us help you out," and Smith promoted himself as "the bail bondsman with a heart."

Writer Russ Million hung out in the office for a day in March 1975, watching the action, listening to Frank's phone calls with underlings assigned to scour the jails for new clients and with employees hunting for bond jumpers. All this action took place while Smith was being investigated by the FBI and the district attorney's office and his bail bond license was under serious threat of revocation.

A lesser human might have fainted from the stress, but Frank was telling jokes, bragging, and posturing. He had loyalists and lackeys who were willing to walk through fire for him. His wife Dorothy was described by Million as a "sharp-tongued, quick-witted woman . . . [who was] clearly an integral part of the operation."

In "Frank Smith, Bail Bonds Businessman," Million seemed to hang on every word of Smith's Texified, narcissistic rap. He quoted a refrain familiar to anyone who knew the man: "My daddy was a Baptist preacher for 43 years. . . . Every time I pass a Baptist church or a wrecking yard, I take off my hat."

Million described Smith as a "large, personable man of al-legedly 'unreformed' moral character" who "admits that he's a red-neck who prefers J&B over marijuana, but he's quick to say he's not racist," the last assertion supposedly attested to by the fact that his auto recycling business, a "ten acre sea of demolished cars slowly being cannibalized by Chicano work crews," was su-pervised by "two men, a Black and a Chicano, who have been with Smith for the 19 years he's been in business."

Two weeks before Russ Million's hangout with Frank, the Tra-vis County Bail Bond Board had conducted a day-long admin-istrative hearing on four main categories of allegations that were serious in nature.[9] Witnesses offered sworn testimony that Smith had solicited acts of arson and theft, coerced the girlfriend of a client into having sex with him before he would obtain her boyfriend's release from jail, and engaged in prohibited methods of promotion and advertisement of his services in the county jail.

One of the star witnesses of the hearing, Cedric Franklin, re-peated the accusations he had given to investigators from the

DA's office, statements that got back to Smith and resulted in Smith making threats against him. It was Frank Smith, he said, who asked him to "burn a brick house on the Lockhart Highway" for $500, with Smith paying for the gasoline. There was more: Smith wanted Franklin to steal three cars and also procure three rings as partial payment for his bail bond fee. Franklin had turned down all these offers, he said. During the hearing, the board also heard testimony that Smith had asked a client to wreck cars in exchange for their bail bond fee. Smith denied all the allegations.

As for the sex solicitation, a woman testified that Smith had forced her "to have sexual intercourse with him to obtain the release of her boyfriend and then to steal and wreck cars and burn a house."[10] The witness was eighteen years old at the time of the incident. The woman testified that she did consent to have sex with Smith only for his promise to secure her boyfriend's release from jail, and that "Smith had made 'indecent' advances once before, but she had refused to comply." By the date of the hearing, the woman and her boyfriend were married.

Smith's attorney in 1975 was Broadus Spivey, a tall, square-jawed Panhandle native and graduate of UT law school who had moved his private practice in Lubbock to Austin in 1971. In later years Spivey became a well-known plaintiff's attorney and, among other honors, served as president of the State Bar of Texas. He was also a great raconteur. During an interview session in 2010, Spivey shared some of the details about the sex-abuse accusation against Smith. The latter was nervous about answering the charge, Spivey said, not so much because of the legalities involved but because the accuser was Black and Dorothy was going to be sitting in the courtroom. "Now, Broadus, you always told me to tell the truth," Smith said. "But Dorothy is going to be sitting in that courtroom." The prospect of Dorothy hearing him describe in court a sexual act he had participated in with a Black woman was simply too much for Smith. He described the dilemma for Spivey in earthy and racist language that does not bear repeating.[11]

Witnesses testified that employees of Sheriff Frank had recommended Frank Smith's bail bond services to them while they were inmates at the county jail. If this sounds like a relatively minor breach of regulations, it was indicative of much more serious violations of protocol and the law.

Statesman reporter John Sutton was convinced that a corrupt arrangement existed between Frank Smith and Sheriff Raymond Frank. Such arrangements were not uncommon, he said, stating that Frank's predecessor, T. O. Lang, had even allowed his favorite bondsman to have an office inside the sheriff's office.

"Frank Smith did support Raymond Frank's election," Sutton said, "and Frank Smith was sort of Raymond Frank's bail bondsman of choice. The bondsmen were not allowed to keep an office there in the sheriff's office, but Frank Smith kind of took up residence on the bench outside the sheriff's office. So he'd go, 'Well, if you need a bondsman, I can take care of you, you just have to put down 15 percent of whatever your bond is.'"

Smith also was alleged to have abused his position by "going off" the bonds of certain clients when it suited him. Bail bondsmen did have the right to cancel, or "motion off," a client's bond for legitimate reasons. Smith claimed that he had only done so when a client had failed to "keep in touch." Smith was the victim here, he claimed, the victim of "a conspiracy of sour grapes." Since day one, he said, "the courthouse clique jailhouse lawyers were out to get me."[12]

Sutton considered it his duty as a journalist to inform the public about the full story of the Two Franks. Bill Cryer, John Sutton, and Dave Mayes were investigating the same thing; so were Carol Fowler and Ron Littlepage at the *Austin Citizen*. Some of the accusations against Smith, such as using the sheriff's

Frank Smith was still on federal parole when his bail bond license was approved. Note that the word "bail" is misspelled on the office window. The glass front was extensively painted with Christmas greetings by a member of the extended gypsy family of Charles Overton (of the notorious Overton Gang); the artist signed his work as "The Knone."

employees to promote his bail bond services, strongly suggested collusion by Sheriff Frank.[13]

The board voted to revoke Smith's license on March 19, 1975. The vote was 4 to 1, with the dissenting vote coming from Sheriff Frank. On the same day Spivey filed a motion for a restraining order in 126th District Court, alleging that the 1974 Bail Bond Act was unconstitutional. That afternoon Judge Jim Myers signed a temporary restraining order, the result being that, in order to revoke Smith's license, the allegations had to be proven.[14] Smith wasted no time crowing that he was "still in business."

When asked about conditions in the county criminal justice system in the 1970s, former judges and other courthouse officials generally shied away from using the term "corruption." Some did, however, offer that relationships too often took precedence over the rule of law. "It's just the way things were done back then," several of them said. Not surprisingly, such relationships were generally aligned with money and power.

Jon Wisser, a district judge for over twenty years, worked under Ned Granger in the county attorney's office beginning in the midseventies. "A few weeks after I was hired to work under Granger, the county attorney, I was told that we were having a big barbecue at the Minton, Burton ranch," he said. The invitation list included Granger and the five assistant county attorneys, plus the district attorney and his six assistants. "So all the assistants and our wives all went out to the Minton, Burton ranch and had a great steak dinner. I kept thinking, 'Well, I thought we were on different sides, but here we are, one big, happy family.'"

Wisser was reluctant to say that such relationships engendered corruption, but he was clearly uncomfortable with the implications. "Minton, Burton had inordinate power, and I didn't think it was healthy," he said. "There wasn't obvious to me a great deal of corruption, or maybe it was hidden," he said. "But there were things done, the way the courthouse operated, and then there was Minton, Burton. They were just a tremendous power in the courthouse, and they had very close relationships with the county attorney, the district attorney, and some of the county commissioners. They had a large say in who was going to be a judge and if you were going to run for election it sure helped to have them on your side."

Wisser acknowledged, "It always bothered me that Mr. Granger had relationships with certain criminal defense firms, and they got preferential treatment over attorneys who didn't have a relationship with Mr. Granger." Particularly troublesome for Wisser were the types of "recommendations" for cases that gave leniency to clients whose attorneys had a "relationship" with Granger, as opposed to clients whose attorneys had no ties to Granger. Long story short: Granger's friends were much less likely to do jail time or pay high fines.

"The whole place was like that," said Wisser, meaning the courthouse, as a culture and a community, or perhaps, as he called it, "a small town." "It was maybe not out and out corruption," he said, "but it wasn't highly ethical."[15]

The county attorney's office prosecuted hot-check writers and other misdemeanor offenses and civil litigation involving the county and its employees. The county attorney was also the official legal representative for the County Commissioners Court and, notably, the bail bond board.[16]

Ned Granger, first elected county attorney in 1967, was credited by colleagues and critics alike with helping modernize county government and smooth the transition of Travis County from a mostly rural area to one that was mostly urban, with a dynamic metropolis at its center that was about to go boomtown. Arnold Garcia Jr., who put in thirty-nine years with the *Statesman* and was a very well-respected editorial-page editor, wrote many critical stories about Granger's shortcomings for the paper, but he also spoke admiringly about Granger's hiring of women and minorities. Granger integrated his staff quietly, Garcia said, without being pressured to do so by mandate and also without making a big deal out of it.[17]

But Granger ignored corruption, according to his critics, and was a slacker about prosecuting cases. Reporters who wrote less-than-flattering articles about him were excoriated. "John Sutton and I did some stories about Ned doing some shady things as county attorney," recalled Bill Cryer. "Ned cornered John in the courthouse one day and said, 'I just want you to tell you guys what it feels like to get up in the morning and see your daughter reading the paper saying that you're a crook. It does not make me very happy.'" Cryer paused for a beat, before adding that the encounter "was not fun."

Ned's daughter Tressa mentioned the times that similarly critical articles appeared in the *Austin Citizen*. She and Ned would drive around Austin, making a stop at every *Austin Citizen* machine. Tressa would hop out of the car, put a dime in the slot, and remove all the copies.

Granger had colorful terms for his critics, too. According to Arnold Garcia, these often consisted of a farm animal plus a verb.[18] He also seems to have been an unapologetic partisan of Frank Smith, a fact that would stain his reputation and add to the harsh criticisms of his last actions in office, which, not surprisingly, he shrugged off without comment. A rampant capitalist who invested heavily in property, Granger also owned part of a pest control company, a fact he sometimes used to comic effect, saying, "Well, if I don't get reelected, I can always go step on bugs."

THIS IS WAR

I liked Frank Smith. He was my buddy, he was
funny, he was a crook, he was a thief, he had every
intention of killing. We remained good friends
although I was in the prosecutor's office when we
convicted him of attempted murder in Fredericksburg. I knew him probably forty years.

—CAROL FOWLER

Frank Smith's feud with Ike Rabb intensified after the first salvage auction of 1976. In his ten-page summary of the troubles
from 1969 through January 1976, Ike Rabb wrote: "Around noon
on Wednesday, January 7 [1976], Frank Smith came into the
Salvage Pool office. I was there and he announced to me that he
was late but that he would like to bid on all the cars including
those that closed out on Tuesday, January 6. These last he said he
would have to call in his bids to the companies." Rabb told him
no. The bidding was closed. "Smith did not like this. He would
not accept the fact that he was too late."

Upon seeing that the bid forms were still sorted in their
pigeon-hole slots, Smith moved toward them, saying, "Are the
bid forms from last week still up there? I'll just take them."

Rabb stepped between Smith and told him that he wasn't
going to get his hands on them, that the bidding was closed, that
he was a day late. Smith argued with him for over an hour, then

drove up and down the lot, trying to identify the cars from the auction by their VIN numbers. He said he was going to contact the insurance companies himself to bid on the cars. "The only way to stop him was to physically restrain him," Rabb wrote, "an act I was not ready to attempt. He drove up and down the lot for thirty or forty minutes, then left to balloon this minor affair into a major crisis."

Later in the day, Smith called Rabb. He'd been calling the companies again, complaining that Rabb was interfering with his business. He also told the insurance companies that Rabb had been stealing the gasoline out of the wrecked cars. Rabb realized Smith was recording their conversation. "There is a physical threat made subtly," Ike wrote. "There is the promise of war."[1]

Later, under oath, Frank Smith would admit to the exact words he said to Ike Rabb: "You can't buck me. . . . This is war, all-out war."[2]

What did Smith mean by "war"? Ike and Jane Rabb didn't know, but they had heard stories about the violence done to previous adversaries of the man. Not that Smith was the type to commit violent acts himself, nor was he ever accused of lighting a single arson fire or holding a gun on a robbery victim. Whenever Smith was charged with such crimes, he was the one who coordinated the acts. He was the criminal mastermind.

Ike Rabb's chronicle, written in concert with Jane Rabb, ends on January 19, 1976. On that day, an adjuster had called Ike to relay a warning: "The adjuster stressed that Smith is crazy, he might just have you blown up. So don't cross him."[3]

Was the adjuster on Ike's side, or was he merely relaying a message for Smith? Ike couldn't tell, but he "strongly" suspected the latter.[4]

By 1976, there were three teenagers in the Rabb household: Denise, Geoff, and Jonathan, aged seventeen, fifteen, and fourteen, respectively. Reneé was eight. Denise and Geoff were enrolled at St. Mark's Academy, a Baptist boarding school in San Marcos a half-hour drive south from Austin, but both siblings usually spent the weekends at home, helping the family business. Jonathan, who had tried St. Mark's briefly and decided "it wasn't his thing," attended Del Valle High School, lived at home, and enjoyed working in the yard, driving a wrecker (in the yard only), and doing other tasks, like staying up some nights, posted in one of the wrecks with a shotgun and on the lookout for poachers.

"Jonathan and I worked side by side," said Geoff. "We both operated equipment, and we all learned to drive at a young age. I was driving when I was in fifth or six grade, and Jonathan was right behind me. We were at the Dalton Road location by then and we were driving wreckers, not on the street, of course, but we would line up the cars for auctioning and one would drive, the other would hook them up with chains, stuff like that."

Teamwork among the brothers, their father, and a brother-in-law extended to taking shifts at night, looking out for thieves. "The dogs were a deterrent," Geoff said, "but we still had a problem with people breaking in and stealing parts off of the cars. Some of them would bring food to give to the dogs, so one or more of us would stay up at night, hiding in the cars or some other spot, so we could apprehend them or foil their attempts. One of the brothers, or our brother-in-law, would take turns, working for several hours, then it would be somebody else's turn. Sometimes we would notice a pattern, and we'd set up surveillance, sitting there with a shotgun. You'd fire off some rounds to scare them off."

Geoff recalled that "one night it was our brother-in-law's turn, and he set up in this van we had. It was what they called a Good Times van, with shag carpet and a bed in back, and he fell asleep." Before long, burglars struck. "They started jacking up the van with him in it. He woke up, came out, and fired a round or two from the shotgun and they ran off. It was funny that he even admitted having fallen asleep. We always gave him hell about that."

Geoff said, "Back when I was twelve years old, Frank used to pay me to remove driveshafts from the cars he bought, a dollar per driveshaft." At the time, he said, he did not know what Frank Smith was capable of doing, only that Smith was insisting on having his way on everything. "We were never able to say, 'OK, that's it with Frank, we're not doing business with him anymore,' because the next thing you know, here's something else he's trying to do."

Denise remembered the day she was working in the office when Frank Smith appeared. "He came into the office and he wanted something," she said. "He looked big and not scared of anything, just a very big presence, a heavy guy who carried himself like a big, confident bad guy. . . . I knew he was a bad guy."

"The Salvage Pool operation was not entirely harmful to Frank," said Ike. "Buyable merchandise was available regularly in one location." Their troubles escalated again after the Rabbs instituted a change from sealed-bid auctions to the open auction method. Bidding happened in the open, alongside the other auction attendees. "No direct dealings with the seller/owner, just competitive bidding with the auction attendees," Ike explained. "Not Frank's style; too open."

HE CAN ALWAYS GO
STEP ON BUGS

Raymond Frank's election for a second term in 1976 must have brought cheer to Frank Smith, who was still smarting from the results of the race for district attorney, when Ronnie Earle knocked out Smith's friend and enabler, two-term county attorney Ned Granger. In the May primary election Earle polled 52 percent of the vote, leaving opponents Ned Granger and Ron Weddington to split the leftovers, 25 percent and 23 percent, respectively. The Republicans were still a niche party in Texas in those days, and as was the case in many local and state elections, the party had not bothered to field a candidate in the general election for district attorney. A third Democratic candidate, former assistant district attorney Charles Craig, had dropped out of the race soon after Earle announced his candidacy.

After his disappointing loss, Granger announced that he would be going into private practice. Later on, Granger and Earle enjoyed a friendly relationship, according to Twila Earle, who remembered that Granger remarked that, with his election loss, he had gotten the better end of the deal, since he ended up making a lot of money, while Earle ended up with a lot of work.

Earle's big finish had followed a late start. His decision to run for DA came very close to the January filing deadline, but once he was in, he worked hard in every precinct, knocking on doors, meeting people. He handed out 67,000 business cards. Leading into the primary, Granger was still expected to win. When the early returns favored Earle, reporter Dave Mayes wrote that Earle was "attempting to break a 22-year tradition in Travis County D.A. races; succession to district attorney has always been from the office of county attorney."[1] Even after Earle was reelected in 1980, some of the courthouse crowd were still "horrified" that he had sidestepped the county attorney conveyor belt to become prosecutor.[2]

Twila Hugley was Earle's executive assistant at the time. She and Earle first met in 1974 when she was working for the Texas senate as a researcher on transportation issues. In 1975, after Earle was appointed chair of the House Transportation Study Committee, he hired Hugley as his administrative assistant. By the end of the year, Hugley was running his capitol office. During that time Hugley had gotten to know Earle well enough that the first time he brought up the subject of running for DA, she was somewhat shocked and told him so. "Ronnie told me he was thinking about running for district attorney, and what did I think about that?" she said. "So I said, 'Are you talking about with the courts and the cops and all that?' And he said, 'Yeah.'"

Hugley was definitely not surprised, however, when Earle, after a short campaign in the early months of 1976, won his decisive victory. "Ronnie was not part of courthouse politics, and he did not get elected on any courthouse politics," she said. "He got elected in spite of them."

Ronnie Earle was excited by the idea of a salaried job that dealt with the law, but at heart he was a reformer. His restless search for the true meaning of justice and how it can be achieved would be a dynamic force for good in Travis County and elsewhere.

Bail bondsmen did not figure into Earle's idea of justice. During the legislative session of 1975, Earle had been a sponsor of HB 1347, legislation that would implement personal bond programs styled after the one in Travis County across the state, with the aim of putting professional bondsmen like Frank Smith out of business.[3] Earle's friend and colleague Sen. Ray Farrabee sponsored a companion bill in the senate. Earle was quoted extensively on the legislation in a two-part series in the *Statesman*. Heavy opposition came from legislators who had day jobs as defense lawyers, as well as the three-hundred-member Texas Association of Professional Sureties, a lobbying organization for the bail bond industry. Spokesman Alvin Day, a former policeman in Houston, called the legislation "socialistic." "When you look at it close, you see it amounts to coddling criminals, spending tax dollars to help criminals," said Day, anxious not to be confused with a humanitarian of the same name, in case there were any. "And don't talk to me about how bad it is for the poor people. Hell, they shouldn't have violated the law if they didn't want to get thrown in jail."

The association succeeded in helping kill the bill, but similar legislation would be proposed during the next session, and it would have the backing of the new Travis County district attorney, Ronnie Earle. With its Dixie Mafia dust-ups and country singers who looked like they rode with a biker gang, Austin in the late 1970s still had some of the rough bark of the frontier and the rat-a-tat-tat of Prohibition–era gangsterism, but as of January 1, 1977, there would be a new district attorney in town, and certain outlaws had good reason to start quaking in their boots.

A IS FOR ARSON

I sure do deny any arson as far as I know about it.
—FRANK SMITH

Monday, October 18, 1976, at three a.m., Ike and Jane Rabb and kids Jonathan and Reneé were jolted awake by an explosion. Scrambling outside in the predawn darkness, they could see fires blazing in various sections of the sprawling twenty-acre yard. The most shocking sight of all was the eviscerated remains of the house trailer office, blown apart by the explosion of the butane tank. The smoldering bits of paper merrily winging upward were ethereal reminders that the trailer was where all the essential business records were kept.

At sunrise they were treated to the sight of their office reduced to "a smoking hulk and steaming ashes," Ike said. Their emotional reaction was a mix of "anger and helplessness," he said, along with "relief that Frank had not hit the house and all of us in it torched as well. Small blessings!"

Early media coverage of the fire did not mention the Rabbs' feud with Frank Smith and his promise of "all-out war."

According to a statement from the sheriff's department, "No evidence has been found that points to arson, but officers are investigating from that standpoint."[1] The short article in the *Statesman*'s "Police Beat" column also stated that the fire "apparently began in a wrecked car on the lot and spread to a trailer which was used as the firm's office." Eight other "spot" fires, which took five firefighting units from three to six a.m. to extinguish, represented the places occupied by eight of the most valuable vehicles on the lot, each one now a total loss. In the days ahead the investigators would issue a statement concluding that the fire had been intentionally set. Ike and Jane Rabb told the sheriff's investigators of their long history of problems with Frank Smith, but from their prior experience with the Two Franks, they had little hope that their complaints would be given much serious attention.

Diesel had been splattered on the most valuable wrecks in the yard, and other evidence suggested that the arsonists' intent was not merely to burn a few cars but the entire yard, meaning all the vehicles and all the structures and equipment belonging to the Austin Salvage Pool. One of the fires had prematurely ignited the butane tank next to the trailer. When the tank exploded, blowing the trailer inside out, it also forced a hasty retreat by the arsonists before they had time to ignite all of the various wrecks they had drenched with diesel fuel. In an ironic twist, the explosion was bad news for both the arsonists and their victims.

Ike and Jane's daughter, Denise Ormand, said she can still hear the sound of her mother running down the hallway of her dormitory in San Marcos at six o'clock that morning. "My mom suddenly appeared at my dorm," she said, "came in and woke me up, saying *He got us! He got us!*" Jane Rabb was always the dramatic one, said Denise, whether the scenario was a happy or sad occasion.

The estimated total damage caused by the fire—$12,000 for the trailer and $5,000 for some of the most valuable wrecks—was misleading. The dollar amount alone was significant, but losing the titles and other documents could have spelled ruin for the Rabbs.

"They were burned to the ground," explained Denise. "They were officing in a mobile home, and they had all this paperwork, but specifically titles, which are secure documents, and that's what you need to move forward in a business like this, and everything was just charcoal," she added. "The titles were in the files, and the files were in the office, and the office was gutted," Ike said in his deep baritone, "and you can't sell a car without the title. It should have wiped us out. It really should have caused us to quit, but that was where my wife Jane worked real hard to replace what records we needed and keep operating at the same time, money came in and out, it was monumental."

They felt physically violated and attacked by the arsonists. The trailer had also contained family records, photos, and belongings. Jane had stored a certain formal gown there, once worn by Denise to a high school prom or Christmas party.

"It was a beautiful dress that Mom had hung for Dad in his office," said Denise. "Mom was always trying to dress me up. She was such a champion for her family and anything she loved. She loved deep, deep, deep."

Geoff and Denise moved back home to Austin the morning of the fire. For the next few months, Geoff and Denise would be commuting to St. Mark's, spending all their free time helping the family recover from the fire. As always, Jane was a tireless worker as well as the family spiritual leader.

"Jane Rabb was the driving force that started the clean-up and organization," wrote Ike in an email. "We all, family, co-workers, Jane's mother and father, and a lot of the insurance community, and some of our buyers, did what they could do to help," he continued. "Much, much agonizing work took place just to reconstruct the inventory files so that the business could survive and continue. The lot contained clues in the form of wrecked autos parked there and whatever legible, burned, and often unclear paper files in the office were available for reconstruction.

"Fortunately, there was an abandoned chicken house nearby that was available for an office," Ike wrote, "so we brought in telephones, desks, chairs, power and even a coffee maker. The local industry was sympathetic and the word got around quickly as to what had happened."

"Mom and Dad already knew that Frank was out to get them," Denise Ormand said. In their minds, there was "never a doubt" about who was responsible for the fire.

One day in late October 1976, Ike Rabb showed up at the *Statesman*'s offices and asked to speak to the editor. One year later, Bill Cryer's boss, city editor Ray Mariotti, recalled his first impressions. "He spoke very softly," Mariotti said of Rabb. "He said Frank Smith was going to hurt him. At least put him out of business, and maybe more. . . . Maybe somebody could do something." Why not just call the police? "Frank Smith brags that he's got the sheriff in his back pocket," said Rabb. "I don't know if he does or not. But I don't feel like I can go to the sheriff for protection."

Mariotti introduced Ike to Bill Cryer. Rabb was familiar with Cryer's reporting, having read volumes in the *Statesman* about Frank Smith's troubles with the bail bond board and other shenanigans. Cryer and Rabb spent the entire afternoon talking in the newsroom. "Ike was having trouble with Frank Smith, a known criminal, and we were looking into his ties with Raymond Frank, but it was problematical as a news story. It was two junkyard dealers having a dispute about business practices. And so we were a little bit hesitant about doing a story unless I could do it and tie it in with Frank Smith and Raymond Frank, and that's what we were really interested in."

Despite those misgivings, Cryer kept working on the story. Six weeks later, the story was still in limbo, but then on the first Friday in December, Mariotti called Cryer at home, telling him he needed to come back to the office. There had been a shooting at the Austin Salvage Pool.

Frank Smith had never been charged with arson before, even though he was a suspect in numerous fire investigations. "Suspicious fires seemed to follow Frank from place to place, but he was never charged until the Austin Salvage Pool case, when he was also charged with being a habitual criminal," Cryer said, referring to charges that were eventually filed in 1977.

There were arson cases in which Smith was the property owner and collected insurance money and at least one fire in which his claim was denied. In certain cases investigators strongly suspected that Smith or his underlings had intentionally caused the fire. In at least one case, the motive was apparent but the case against Smith was never proven. Finally, there was documented proof that Smith associated with criminals who did not mind committing arson for money, proof that he had hired arsonists at least once, and proof that he tried but failed to hire someone for a job on at least one other occasion.

The office at Frank Smith Auto Parts burned down September 14, 1968, when Frank was on appeal bond for his conviction on car-theft conspiracy charges. The timing is curious. A photograph taken onsite was published in the *Statesman* two days after the fire. The caption provides the only details about the fire that could be found. "FIRE DAMAGE—Members of the Pflugerville Fire Department and Boy Scout volunteers battled a blaze late Saturday night at Frank Smith's Auto Parts, 9727 N. Interregional," reads the text. "Though an office building was destroyed, the firemen did save a nearby warehouse. The blaze was reported about 9:30 p.m. Firemen said the office was a total loss when they arrived."[2]

In July 1975 Royal Globe Insurance Co. denied Smith's $15,500 claim on a house at 1818 Adina Street in East Austin after the fire marshal's office determined the house had been intentionally set ablaze on February 10 and again on March 8 of that year. City and state fire marshal offices investigated. A fire inspector named Jack Kennedy gave a statement to the *Statesman*: "We believe it's arson, that the fires were intentionally set. We're still looking for enough evidence to pin it on somebody."

Smith was asked to respond. "I sure do deny any arson as far as I know about it," he said.[3]

A *Statesman* article from the previous March contained more suborning-of-arson claims. In a hearing concerning Smith's lawsuit against the Travis County Bail Bond Board, witness Cedric Franklin testified "that Frank Smith asked him to burn a house on the Lockhart Highway for $300, or $500 if he 'did a good job to it,'" and volunteered to buy the gasoline. Franklin also said that he'd been threatened after giving information about Smith to the DA's office. Smith denied everything.[4]

Letisha Taylor, Frank's daughter, denied that her father ever burned any houses down. He was a person who had come to the aid of fire victims numerous times. He had pulled a neighbor from his burning house and saved his car, too. Her father was the kind of person who "went around like Robin Hood, helping people that had deaths, fires, illness, divorce . . ." According to Taylor, her father gave thousands of dollars of cash and countless automobiles to people in need.

One of the most troubling incidents in which Frank Smith was suspected involved the suburban home at 11401 Hunters Lane, directly across the street from the Smith residence. An explosion rocked the neighborhood at approximately eight a.m. on the morning of September 20, 1975. Air Force Master Sgt. Calvin Walls had just purchased the home from Charles Hunter, who, like Walls, worked at Bergstrom Air Force Base. The sale had closed just days earlier, and the Hunters were in the process of moving out. The Hunters were white. The Walls would have been the first Black family to move into the all-white neighbor-hood. The county investigation determined that the fire was intentionally set.[5]

At the time Frank's daughter Letisha was fifteen years old, living at home with her family. "We were all still in bed when it happened," she said. "I know folks thought Dad had it done. Many other folks were verbal about them selling to a Black fam-ily," but she said she never heard her father discuss it.

County fire chief Lee Basore spoke with the *Statesman* about the two partially filled gasoline cans found on the site, along with other evidence that the fire had been deliberately set. A seven-inch strip of burned grass led from the house to the street. Basore felt that although the arsonist was probably not a "com-plete amateur," the job was a "very sloppy" one.[6]

Larry Dowling was one of the many lawyers who represented Frank Smith over the years, and, more important, Dowling was a frequent visitor and confidant during his client's last years, when he had less reason to cover his tracks. When asked about the Hunters Lane fire in an interview, Dowling said, "Well, I'm sure it was Frank. If Frank didn't want them there, I'm sure he did it." When pressed for an answer about the other fires, par-ticularly the insurance fires, Dowling laughed. What is so funny about arson? asked the interviewer. Dowling replied, "I know that Frank preferred insurance money over any other money."

THE ROBBERY

I never saw the gun in the man's hand. I never saw
anything but his face. That's as far as I got. Then
the next thing I knew there was this *pow, pow, pow*.
I never heard the shotgun blast.

—JANE RABB, IN "THE SALVAGE YARD SHOOT
OUT," *TEXAS SUN*, JANUARY 1977

The phone at the Salvage Pool office kept ringing. Insurance
industry contacts, adjusters, salvage buyers, and other people
they dealt with were calling with messages of support and offers
of assistance. Instead of bringing the Rabbs ruin and defeat, the
fire strengthened their relationships in the industry. "They all
banded together and helped re-create the records that we had
lost, helped us get back on our feet again and enabled us to be
successful," Ike said.

Not that everything was rosy. Four days after the fire, Frank
Smith filed a lawsuit against Ike Rabb and the Austin Salvage
Pool in 126th District Court.[1] Styled as *Frank Smith vs. Isaac
Rabb*, the petition claimed that the Rabbs' refusal to do business
with him was a violation of the Sherman Anti-Trust Act and the
Deceptive Trade Act. The petition also asserted that the Rabbs'
protocol of selling wrecks before the new title had been issued
was a violation of the Texas Certificate of Title Act.

The latter complaint referred to what was then a common business practice. When an insurance company sold a wrecked car through a brokerage, they guaranteed the vehicle had a clear title with the understanding that obtaining the new title from the motor vehicle registration division generally took about sixty days. Waiting until the new salvage title had been issued would cause a delay in the sale of a vehicle by many weeks, and no one really wanted that.

One week later, Ike and Jane Rabb were again served papers. Rudolph Robinson, the yard manager at Frank Smith & Sons Auto Parts, was also suing them, his chief complaint being an accusation of racial discrimination.[2] "Petitioner is a resident, black citizen of Travis County, Texas," the petition stated, "and has been and is such at all times pertinent hereto." In every case where the respondents were mentioned, the word "white" was inserted as a descriptor, written by an unknown hand.

Robinson's suit alleged that the Rabbs were "maliciously" conspiring to bankrupt Robinson's employer to "render destitute, jobless, and homeless Rudolph Robinson, his wife, and minor children . . . to effectively discriminate against and economically lynch and bankrupt this black Petitioner, Rudolph Robinson, and his family and to destroy and castrate this black citizen's good name, reputation and credit." Robinson also accused Isaac Rabb of trying to "blackmail" him.

By this point, the Rabb family was accustomed to Smith pulling "one shenanigan after another," but being sued by Robinson still came as a surprise, according to Denise Ormand.

"I hardly remember Rudolph at all," said Ike. "We had no run-ins with him. We mostly had phone conversations with him. On rare occasions he would come by to look at one of the gems that Frank had bought, trying to figure out how to get it over there."

Unfortunately, District Judge Herman Jones granted the injunction sought by Smith, the result being that the Rabbs were legally bound to do business with him.[3] At that point the yard at

Austin Salvage Pool was literally clogged with dozens of wrecks that Smith had bought previously but had never paid for. Ike phoned Smith and gave him a deadline to pick up and pay for between thirty and fifty wrecks. If he did not follow through by the end of the week, the wrecks would be sold to other bidders at the next auction.

Wednesday passed peacefully, as did Thursday, and Friday morning, too. It was cold that day at the yard, the low temperatures just above freezing, and inside the chicken coop office, any warmth generated by the little electric space heater was quickly dissipated every time the door opened. After lunch, Ike and Jane were working in the office with two wrecker drivers and an office assistant.

The teenage Rabbs were at school and eight-year-old Reneé was at a friend's birthday party. The later it got, the more it looked as though Frank was not going to show. Everyone felt relieved. But then at 3:45 that afternoon, the sun sitting low in the sky, someone spotted a light green Cadillac coming down the long drive from Dalton Lane. The big car lumbered slowly, making its way to the office. Behind the wheel was the last person in the world they wanted to see.

Ike and Jane endured almost two hours of the Frank Smith treatment: boasting, bickering, suddenly making up his mind, then changing it again. Once the decision was final, there was a lot of work to do. Jane filled out the necessary papers at such a rate that the completed forms were piling up on the floor. The total bill came to $15,000. Frank forked over $15,000 in cash from his bag, accepted his receipt, and, at about 5:45 p.m., spooned his bulk into the tortured driver's seat of his Cadillac and steered back down the long driveway to Dalton Lane.

The sun had retired for the day; the last remnants peeked through the tall Johnson grass and live oaks in the flattened outskirts of town. Jonathan Rabb offered to go lock the gate.

Keith New, the teenage son of Luther New, hopped in the cab of a wrecker to ride with Jonathan. A few minutes later at least two witnesses from the neighborhood noticed the flickering head-lights of a 1975 black-over-yellow Ford LTD bumping down the drive from Dalton Lane, then stopping alongside Frank's green Cadillac. Witnesses estimated that the two cars stopped for ten to fifteen seconds, time enough for a brief dialogue.

Jonathan and Keith found their way blocked by the Ford. A man wearing a monkey mask and jumpsuit got out, jammed a revolver in Jonathan's ribs, and ordered him to back up, all the way to the office. The driver of the Ford wore a ski mask and a jumpsuit, and he, too, had a pistol. The monkey mask rode with the boys, Jonathan driving in reverse, his heart in his throat, con-vinced that this man intended to murder everybody, himself, his father, and his mother included. But he felt helpless.

Inside the office were Ike and Jane, plus two employees, Luther New and Mary Knickerson, and a friend named James Keeling who'd just happened to drop by that day. Luther was on the phone, talking to the sheriff's office about getting an escort to the bank.

Here we return to the incident described in the introduction: a man, not very tall, entered the office wearing a rubber monkey mask and jumpsuit and in one of his gloved hands he held a gun.

Ike Rabb described the mayhem that ensued. "He just said, *Gimme the money*, and I went nuts, I just headed for the shotgun, because I was sitting to the right of the shotgun, maybe about six or seven feet, and he blazed away, but unfortunately, he wasn't very good with housekeeping his automatic, because it jammed, stuck after he got off three shots."

Even in that terrible moment, with 9-millimeter slugs danc-ing around their heads, most of the people in that room could have told you who was behind the current mayhem. "As to the robbery, Jane and I never doubted who was behind it," Ike said. "Never any doubt. Only Frank knew when and where the money would be available. We figured even he would be too crazy to try it, but I placed the 20-gauge on the shelf by my desk in the chicken house, just in case."

Ike fired both barrels, adding much weight to the terrible, ear-splitting sound pressure. The 20-gauge shotgun is a lighter firearm than a 12-gauge, with less recoil, an effective and popular choice for hunting waterfowl.

An action hero Ike was not. "I never thought about it," he said. "It was just the end of a very frustrating time with the whole business, and when he walked in, I just lost my head. I should never have reacted at all." The next few words were garbled by static, but the interviewer thought it sounded like Ike had said, "I shouldn't have shot him." When asked to clarify his previous statement, he said, "What I was saying is that I should not have, I just, I kind of lost my head. I just went for the gun to get him."

Ike said something similar in an interview with the *Texas Sun*: "It was simply a reaction-type thing," he said. "If I'd had time to think, I don't guess I'd have done anything. I just moved when I saw him. . . . I've always been kind of a fumble-footed, fumble-fingered kind of guy, never really well coordinated at all."

In contrast, Jane Rabb's description of the event still buzzed and rattled with the high drama of the moment. "I could have reached out and touched him," she said. "I was just staring into this mask trying to figure out what it was. I screamed. I didn't know I screamed, but the wrecker driver in the yard said he heard this horrible scream, 'Oh my God!' That's my favorite expression, I guess, when I'm scared. I never saw the gun in the man's hand. I never saw anything but his face. That's as far as I got. Then the next thing I knew there was this *pow, pow, pow*. I never heard the shotgun blast."[4]

The monkey-mask bandit lay dying on the floor, his trigger-finger still pulling on the jammed gun. Ike took the gun away, a 9-millimeter pistol, cleared the jam, and belatedly remembered that he had his own pistol in his back pocket. He gave that one to Luther, leaving him in charge of the bandit, went outside, saw a robber with a gun pointed at him, and then he saw another masked gunman. They shot at Ike and missed. Ike shot at them and missed. They ran away. Ike went back inside to check on everybody.

Doyne Bailey, an APD homicide detective, was out in his patrol car near Bergstrom Air Force Base (present-day Austin-Bergstrom International Airport), less than five minutes away from ASP, when the call came over dispatch. He arrived at the scene about the same time as a city police officer named Claude Ricks.

"We gravitated to the office and found the dead guy, and the only other people that were there were Isaac Rabb and Luther New," said Bailey. "While I was there Sheriff Frank showed up along with the news crew. I'm sure they just arrived at the same time but you know, he brought the news crew into the little office and started explaining what happened, and it just struck me wrong. We weren't even starting our investigation yet, and it was just inappropriate in my mind."

Sheriff Frank's behavior, as Bailey saw it, was classic Raymond Frank, another example of his need to be "front and center." Jane Rabb was going "a mile a minute," and Ike Rabb seemed relatively unaffected, and that was typical, too.

"Isaac was probably as cool as anybody I've ever known," Bailey said. "If he ever got excited, he never let anybody know it, and Jane was like a rolling ball of butcher knives. She was always going at full throttle. She didn't have a slow-down gear at all."

The city detectives stuck around to lend a hand, though Dalton Lane was outside city limits, making the crime scene the sheriff's jurisdiction. Members of the Organized Crime Unit, including their top detective, Lt. Bobby Simpson, arrived within a few minutes of the robbery report.

Justice of the Peace Bob Perkins, a native of Eagle Pass and the first bilingual judge elected in Travis County, also responded to

APD Homicide detective Doyne Bailey (*left*) and Chief Deputy Jim Collier at the Austin Salvage Pool crime scene. The cramped space inside the tiny office left little room to step around the dead body of Willie McKnight.

the call. "I happened to be on duty that night," he said. "It was a pretty exciting event." After getting the call Perkins drove out to the Salvage Pool, arriving there before Sheriff Frank. After being apprised of the situation by two sheriff's deputies, Perkins said, "Let's roll him over and find out who he is. Have you looked in his pockets yet?" The deputies said no, that Sheriff Frank had told them not to not touch the body or do anything else until he got there.

"Which was kind of strange," Perkins said. "It was not usual procedure."

Sheriff Frank and the media arrived. The robber was rolled over, his mask carefully removed and scooped onto the end of Frank's flashlight, all for the benefit of everyone crowded into the former chicken condominium, but especially for the photographers and TV camera operators.

Perkins wrote his report and drove to his office at 2201 Post Road. While completing his report, he decided to place a call to Bob O. Smith, the lame-duck DA. "I wanted him to know about this deal from the get-go," said Perkins. "For years there'd been a lot of rumors that Frank Smith had the sheriff in his pocket. So, I called Bob Smith and told him what had happened."

Bob Smith told Bob Perkins he appreciated the heads-up.[5]

Bobby Simpson's officers told John Sutton they were shocked to see Raymond Frank "immediately go over to the robbers' vehicle and get his fingerprints all over the place." The cops watched "in horror," convinced that the sheriff was intentionally destroying evidence. "That's what they thought," Sutton said. "He was all over the vehicle. He opened the door and looked in the glove box, got his prints on all the windows, put his hands all over the steering wheel and the exterior."

Nonetheless, the search yielded some important clues that would help identify the robbers, including fingerprints that the sheriff had failed to obliterate and a coat with a bottle of pills in the pocket that had been prescribed for Aymon R. Armstrong, an ex-policeman from that gravitational center of underworld crime, the Haltom City suburb of Fort Worth.

Bill Cryer had gone home for the day, but a call from his editor, Ray Mariotti, yanked him back to the newspaper office and the frantic pace of the crime beat. "You'd better get down here," said Mariotti. "There's been a robbery out at the Salvage Pool and somebody's been shot."

Cryer, along with several other reporters, had been investigating and writing about Frank Smith for at least a year. During that same time they had also been investigating Sheriff Frank, whose bail bond policies always seemed to favor Smith.

Cryer drove back downtown to the newspaper office, then located at Fourth and Guadalupe, and started making phone calls. "The police reporter, who was this young man, didn't know that I was already working on a story," recalled Cryer. "He was really, really pissed at the city editor for calling me in to do this story, and I don't think he ever forgave me."

Cryer drove out to the crime scene. The Salvage Pool was thick with reporters and cops from several different agencies. Cryer spent a couple of hours talking to Ike and Jane Rabb in their kitchen. "Ike, of course, was completely calm," Cryer said. "I've never met a man like him before. Jane, of course, was upset, nervous and angry. She was the one saying, '*Goddamn, Frank Smith did this. . . I should've shot that SOB . . .*' and despite Ike's cool, he was saying essentially the same thing. That it had to be Frank Smith."

Cryer also spoke to Frank Smith on the phone that night to complete his story for the morning paper, in which Smith denied having anything to do with the robbery. Cryer's story pointed out that the robbers had struck just minutes after Smith left; but Smith claimed that he did not "see anybody or hear anything" and then floated a fever-dream theory of his own. "Something stinks about this," Smith said. "I was set up out there. . . . I think this is terrible. It was a miracle that I escaped. My underworld sources tell me that I was very, very fortunate to have gotten away."

Frank's days of "getting away" were running short, however. The Rabbs weren't the only people convinced that he was behind the robbery.

"Everybody thought that," said Cryer in an interview. "Everybody knew Frank Smith had paid these people." When it was announced in the media that one of the dead man's pockets held several $100 bills and other denominations for a total of $650, a large swathe of Austin population presumed that that money had come from Frank Smith.

"It was pretty obvious, from what Ike Rabb said, what the police said, and just the basic facts there on the ground," Cryer said. "The robbers showed up just as Frank Smith left, and Frank had just given the Rabbs $15,000 cash. I think everyone was dumbfounded because Frank Smith was supposed to be this large criminal. How could he have done something so stupid?"

"But we couldn't report it that way," Cryer explained. "The paper's lawyer wouldn't let me write that kind of story." Armed with an overabundance of incriminating facts, Cryer dealt with the restrictions imposed on him by the *Statesman*'s legal office by writing an impressively tight crime narrative, woven from beginning to end with background information that all but indicted Frank Smith. In the first two paragraphs of "Junkyard Owner Shotguns Robber," excerpted below, the italicized words [emphasis added] were winking acknowledgements of the reporter's intent.

A robber *who apparently knew* that $15,000 had just been delivered to an auto salvage yard east of Austin was shotgunned to death Friday afternoon in an exchange of gunfire with the owner of the firm.

The robber and his two companions *had just missed the man* who delivered the money, Frank H. Smith, a prominent Austin bail-bondsman and auto salvage dealer. The dead man's accomplices were still at large early Saturday.[6]

Apparently, in the mind of Frank Smith, hiring people to rob the $15,000 he just had handed to Ike Rabb a few minutes earlier seemed like a sound plan.

The name of the dead robber was Robert Willie McKnight. In a mug shot taken a few years earlier, he had short, dark hair and black horn-rimmed glasses that made him look nerdy and forlorn. More recently McKnight had adopted the trademark 1970s outlaw look: long, shaggy hair and salt-and-pepper whiskers. Dead at thirty-eight, McKnight had a criminal record going back at least to 1953 when, as a fifteen-year-old youth offender on probation, he stole a car and led police on a hundred-mile-per-hour chase. Given a reprieve instead of a term at reform school, he got in a knife fight on his first day back at school. The "freckle faced boy" described in earlier accounts became a fixture in the Haltom City underworld: an accomplished safecracker, burglar, armed robber, drug smuggler, and member of an infamous criminal outfit known as the Walter Mark Flanagan burglary gang.[7]

McKnight had served six years in the federal pen, from 1954 to 1960, for transporting stolen cars across state lines, a criminal activity he had in common with Frank Smith.[8] McKnight had gone back to federal prison in 1962 for another two years, this time on a conviction of counterfeiting securities. In recent years McKnight had owned a used car dealership in Haltom City. He had borrowed the Ford LTD back in August to sell on consignment.[9]

Meanwhile, investigators were focusing their attention on two other suspects: Aymon Armstrong, who had left his coat and medicine behind, and Guy Henry Collins, whose fingerprints had been found inside the car. Both Collins and Armstrong were friends of McKnight's. Both were from Haltom City. McKnight and Collins were used car dealers. Armstrong was an ex-cop. They hung out together. One source was quoted saying that Armstrong and McKnight were "buddies from way back."

Aymon Armstrong was bringing groceries home to his wife and daughter on Saturday afternoon, December 4, when he was arrested by Fort Worth robbery detectives. He was charged with

By the time of his arraignment on charges of aggravated robbery in December 1976, Aymon Armstrong had fallen a long way from the previous year, when he was a decorated hero cop in Tarrant County. He had yet to hit bottom.

attempted capital murder and was transported to Austin, where he was arraigned on the same charge and held in the county jail on $500,000 bond. On Tuesday, December 7, he was re-arraigned on a charge of aggravated robbery, an offense that carried the same sentence of from five to ninety-nine years, or life. Bail was reduced to $100,000.[10]

People who lived and worked in the Dalton Lane neighborhood had been able to identify Armstrong from pictures that investigators showed them. In order to reach Dalton Lane or any other public road in that part of town, the fugitive gunmen had to make their way through weeds, bushes, and ditches, emerging somewhere on a road in that rural/industrial patch of town where a lone pedestrian would have been an unusual sight.

Only a year earlier Armstrong had been known as a decorated, heroic Tarrant County detective, a handsome, square-jawed, blue-eyed member of the elite Organized Crime Intelligence Unit, better known by its sexier name, Metro Squad.[11] Armstrong had been awarded the county's medal of honor for his actions in a shootout with a bank robbery suspect in 1971. His reputation and career stepped into an open elevator shaft, however, when an investigation by a private citizens' commission confirmed that he and several of his colleagues had been working overtime for some of the biggest crooks in North Texas. Armstrong organized a drug raid, complete with seven pounds of marijuana that was planted in an ex-con's residence. Why? As punishment for flipping the bird at an assistant district attorney. Armstrong also had been working security for illegal gambling at the westside crib of Curtis Glyn Garrett, one of the biggest gamblers in Texas. Back in the 1960s he'd been a running buddy of Austin's jocular ex-Longhorn gang leader Timmy Overton.

Armstrong was asked to resign in lieu of being fired. Two other detectives were reassigned. The Metro Squad was disbanded.

Some of Armstrong's former colleagues were not surprised by the revelations. "Not only is he an outlaw now, he always was one," said another. "Even when he was on the force, he was always doing things to help the opposition." Twila Earle remembered Armstrong's "scary eyes." "He had sort of an aura," she said. "Aymon's eyes had a real cold, metallic, edgy thing to them."

Armstrong got a private investigator's license and took out ads in the *Fort Worth Star-Telegram*. His office and McKnight's used car lot were just ten blocks apart.[12]

Guy Henry Collins, forty-two, owned a used car lot on E. Belknap Street in Haltom City. On January 2, 1976, witnesses claimed to have seen Collins arguing with a customer over a down-payment on a car. At some point Collins pulled out a .38 revolver and shot the customer in the head. Charged with murder, Collins was released on a $10,000 bond. Collins had several other charges pending as well, including a handgun violation, a federal charge for possession of amphetamines with intent to distribute, and, finally, a case for possession of a quantity of methaqualone, better known back in the day as Quaalude, Sopor, and disco biscuit.

The way Collins told it, he first learned about the Austin Salvage Pool robbery from a newspaper story on Wednesday, December 8. After seeing his photo and reading that he had been charged with aggravated robbery, he surrendered to authorities in Tarrant County and was driven to Austin by deputies from Travis County. By the time the party crested the incline on I-35 south of Round Rock, where gentle hills parted to reveal the state capitol dome and UT Tower, Collins had been indicted for aggravated robbery by the county grand jury, his bond set at $500,000.

Investigators would spend the remaining days of 1976 gathering more evidence against Armstrong while trying to figure out how Guy Collins had been involved, if he had been involved at all. Collins provided phone records and witnesses to prove he was at home in Haltom City, not in Austin, at the time of the robbery attempt. He stood in a lineup, and the witnesses failed to identify him, yet here he was, paying $12 for a carton of cigarettes and toiletries, which he considered "pretty damn high."[13]

The best thing about the case against Collins was the jokey headline for the *Statesman* article on December 16: "Robbery Alibi 'Won't Hold Up.'" When Bill Cryer came to interview Collins in his cell on the sixth floor of the county courthouse, Collins strenuously maintained his innocence, saying that somebody had made "a big mistake." "People up there told me they figured I'd be out in two or three days," he said. "They better be right." Collins told Cryer about the seven people in Fort Worth who would verify his whereabouts on the day of the robbery. He conceded that he had been in the Ford LTD, but it was on December 1 in a garage, not on a quick trip to Austin with McKnight on December 3. "I didn't do anything," he insisted. "If I was going to do anything I wouldn't have touched anything and left my fingerprints."[14]

Collins and Armstrong just barely missed each other. Collins was still being transported to Austin when the county grand jury indicted Armstrong, and as soon as that was made official, the ex-cop posted $100,000 bail and lit a shuck out of town.[15]

Reporters Bill Cryer and Dave Mayes were told by Sheriff Frank that a Fort Worth man named Curtis Glyn Garrett had signed over 575 acres of ranchland worth about $250,000 to stand as surety for Armstrong's bail. The reporters admitted that, so far, they knew very little about Garrett except that he had flown in a private plane from Las Vegas to Fort Worth to make the bond, after which Armstrong's attorneys flew to Austin in a private plane to deliver it.

Some of Garrett's escapades in the 1960s are covered in my book *1960s Austin Gangsters: Organized Crime that Rocked the Capital.* Acquitted in the 1968 bank burglary conspiracy trial in Del Rio, Garrett emerged in the 1970s as a prominent Fort Worth gambler, high-flying nightclub owner, and pimp.[16] At some point he picked up a title as "The Meanest Man in Fort Worth," but he could be generous, too. When it appeared that one of Armstrong's accomplices in the Salvage Pool robbery had been cooperating with the police and was likely to testify against Armstrong, Garrett offered to have him killed.[17]

Collins managed to arrange a deal with two Fort Worth bondsmen for bail (which cost him personally $15,000, he said), and left Austin for Haltom City with a little over a week to do Christmas shopping for his wife and mother-in-law. Time moved on, Collins resumed his criminal career in Fort Worth, and although the case against him remained on the books, his name was rarely spoken again in Austin, and his case never came to trial.[18]

So far, Frank Smith had not been questioned. Reporters had been asking the sheriff questions about Smith ever since the night of the robbery. After a week of being hounded by the press, Sheriff Frank said Frank Smith would be questioned "undoubtedly, and we'll question anybody else who we think might know something." The sheriff tried to shoot down the "allegations" and "innuendos" that he and Frank Smith were friends. "There is no involvement between myself and Frank Smith in this," he said. "We will do anything we can to carry out our duties. I think this is a very complex case and it may take a little time to unwind it."[19]

Friday, December 17, a full two weeks after the aborted robbery, Smith appeared for an interview at the sheriff's office. At his side was Broadus Spivey, the lawyer who had filed Smith's litigation against the Rabbs and represented him in the case before the bail bond board.

Sheriff Frank was not present. Chief Deputy Jim Collier asked the questions. Afterward, Collier refused to divulge any of the answers with reporters Cryer and Mayes, but he seemed downright cheerful about the visit. "It was a good clean interview," he told them. "He answered the questions we put to him, and, I think, truthfully. Nobody was uptight. It was pretty congenial all the way around."[20]

POWER

There were terrible stories. There were these two
different bodies found while Frank was out of jail,
guys who'd jumped bail on Frank, found with a
funeral wreath next to each body. That may have
been an apocryphal story that Frank made up to
scare people, but I was ready to believe it. I was
ready to believe anything bad he could do because
he was a cruel man and very, very powerful.

—CAROL FOWLER

Bill Cryer spent the week before Christmas 1976 working on
a detailed and damning portrait of Frank Smith. "A Man with
Power: Austin Outlaws and Elite Know Frank Smith," was published Sunday, December 26, on page one, above the fold.

Even after a gap of several decades, pictures of Frank Smith
from that time hit Bill Cryer like a chill wind. "I remember those
cold, appraising eyes, always taking your measure, probing—
where to slip the knife, fulfill the secret desire," he said in an interview. "But there was something basically missing in Frank,
some limit that put you on guard." He compared that limit to
the scent a fox emits that alerts its prey to danger. Perhaps it was
a vestigial remnant of conscience left over from Smith's Baptist
upbringing.

"A Man with Power" is a classic piece of big-city crime beat reportage, written at the interesting juncture when Austin was about to leap from medium-sized city to booming modern metropolis. Cryer structured the story so that it begins like an exposé, packing it with noirish touches worthy of Raymond Chandler.

All kinds of people know Frank Hughey Smith: waiters, lawyers and politicians; mechanics, legislators and judges; 11th Street whores, pimps and dope pushers; Baptist preachers and reporters," he wrote. "He's known in the very best and the very worst places in town. He's known as a generous friend and an unrelenting foe. He's known for his affable good humor and salty tales. Frank Smith is also known for his power. He may be a rascal, he may be an honest businessman, but above all else, Frank Hughey Smith is a man who knows power.

After investigating and writing about Smith for at least a year, Cryer had spent many hours face-to-face with his subject. In one interview Cryer said, "I would go over to his [bail bond] office a lot. I'd go there and he'd sit there and bullshit with you for hours, if you let him."

"His office was furnished in imported, heavy Mexican wood-work, just like you might expect a Mafia don to have in his office," Cryer continued. "There was a big bulletin board in the waiting room with all these news stories from all over the country about people who had been mysteriously found dead. One of them was a burned corpse found in Los Angeles. I asked Frank about it, and he said, 'Oh, those are my former clients.' He laughed and said, 'I just put those pictures up there so that my future clients will know that they really shouldn't jump bail on me.' I never knew whether he was serious or it was an instance of Frank's sense of humor."

Cryer vividly remembered the Sunday afternoon when Frank invited him to take a ride in his Cadillac. They drove from one end of Austin to the other, Smith stopping periodically to point out various buildings and properties that he owned, saying, "I own that, I own this. . . . I own that over there, too." After viewing a considerable amount of real estate, Frank articulated the point of the tour. "I just want you to know, Bill," he said, "when you write these stories about me, I'm a man of means."

"I realize that, Frank."

The last stop on the tour was the wrecking yard. "He gave me a tour of his operation on North I-35," Cryer said. "It was huge and state-of-the-art and well maintained. It was very impressive. And in the back of the yard was this giant car crusher, and I remember this just like it was yesterday, sitting in his Cadillac, looking at this huge crusher, and Frank said, 'Now, Bill, that thing, you can put a whole car in there and crush it down to a cube, about one foot on each side. And if I wanted to, I could put a person in a car and crush it and they wouldn't find him, ever.'"

"He looked at me," Cryer recalled, "and he said, 'You might want to keep that in mind. I don't care what you write about me, Bill, but by God, it better be the truth.' And then he took me back to my car."

In "A Man with Power," Cryer lists six arson fires in which the primary suspect was Frank Smith. Some of those cases have previously been mentioned in these pages, but not the case in which Frank's father's old church exploded and burned in July 1975. The *Statesman* article has Smith responding to the arson question with a shrug, followed by "I don't really know anything about those other fires . . . but I can tell you about the church fire."

Cryer wrote: "The church, he said, was sold by him to a preacher after he had made sure all of his father's former congregation who had money tied up in the church had been paid off in full." Smith told him, "Those people had fed and clothed me all my life. They didn't lose any money on it. They got back 100 per cent." Cryer wrote that Smith "claims the person who bought the property got more in insurance than he paid Smith for the property. Other than that, he says, he is ignorant of the fire."

Let us unpack that paragraph. A church Frank Smith once owned was destroyed by arson, but the new owner got paid off by the insurance company and even made a profit after buying it from Smith, so everything turned out rosy. Smith assured Cryer that "those people" (the congregation) got all their money back, too. Other than that, he knew nothing about the fire. Was that supposed to make him sound innocent?

The final third of "A Man with Power" concerns the highly suspect relationship between Frank Smith and Sheriff Raymond Frank. It poses the notion that Sheriff Frank was "overly solicitous of the welfare of Frank Smith's bail bond business," a supposition that had "wide currency" around the courthouse, where it seemed that "everything that Raymond Frank has done about the bail bond system has been to the benefit of only one person: Frank Smith."

The Two Franks were vocal opponents of the personal bond office. When the Travis County Bail Bond Board voted unanimously in favor of revoking Smith's license, Raymond Frank was the only abstaining member.

Cryer also came up with a scoop about the relationship between the Two Franks that merited a sidebar to "Power." During their tour of Smith's wrecking yard, Cryer had spotted what he described as a "beautifully restored Model T Ford, completely redone." Intrigued, he whipped open his reporter's notebook and jotted down the license number. Later, back at the office, he called DPS to run down the name on the registration. The vehicle was registered to Raymond Frank, and the sale had been consummated in 1972, the year that Frank was elected county sheriff.

Cryer: "So I went to Raymond Frank and I said, 'I thought you said you don't have any connection with Frank Smith.' And he said, 'I don't. I hardly even know the man.' I said, 'Why do they have a Model T Ford up there in his junkyard and the license plate says it belongs to you?'"

In "Smith Bought Frank's Car," Cryer wrote that Sheriff Frank "bristled angrily" when he was asked about the vintage auto. "Does that make me look bad?" he asked Cryer. "It was a perfectly legal sale," he said, asserting that he was a longtime vintage car buff and had purchased the Model T in the 1950s.

"I am not linked with Frank Smith, it's that simple," the sheriff told Cryer. "Frank Smith never contributed to my campaign, and he never gave me a penny. . . . I don't like to be gutted in the newspaper over something as cheap as this."[1]

As mentioned in a previous chapter, Frank's contention that Smith never contributed to his campaign was refuted by numerous sources.

The sheriff was so angry when Cryer asked about the car that it made the reporter "a little nervous." The case of nerves lasted through Christmas, he said. The holiday was "spoiled" for him that year by his fears about possible repercussions after the two stories were published. He dreaded writing a follow-up, he said, because it would be difficult finding sources over the holidays. Making holiday plans with his wife and their two young children, ages three and four, was no fun, either, because any plan was subject to last-minute cancellation in case some "ugly reaction" to his reporting necessitated a journalistic response.

As it turned out, the year ended not with a bang but a silent whimper. The way Cryer sees it now, "A Man with Power" fell into "the news equivalent of a black hole between Christmas and New Year's."[2] Nothing much happened: no irate phone calls, no severed equine head left on his pillow.

Turning self-reflective, Cryer said that reading the stories today gives him "a sense of incredulous unreality." "These stories were written by a younger me who was excited—thrilled, really—chasing after slivers of facts in a spongy world ruled by liars and upside-down people who kept loaded guns under car seats, lived in dingy motel rooms and did unspeakably cruel things to friends and strangers—while in my world we watched Mary Tyler Moore and took our kids to Barton Springs. These scribbles remind me, now a half century gone, that such a ridiculous world existed—and still does, somewhere. And, I thank God that I am no longer on that strange and peculiar beat."

The "strange and peculiar beat" turned even more bizarre in 1977, as Cryer and a handful of other dedicated reporters tracked each weird new development in the case against Frank Hughey Smith Sr., the junkyard/bail bond king.

STAR TIME

If anybody has anything on me, they ought to take it to the grand jury. They ought to do that rather than go around talking about a working man. They ought to put up or shut up.

—FRANK SMITH

Monday morning, January 31, 1977, the front steps of the Travis County Courthouse played host to a buzzing throng of reporters from area newspapers and radio and television stations. In the cold wind and drizzle, the cream-colored limestone slabs of the eastern façade of the courthouse, built in PWA Moderne style in 1931, took on a dark, somber tone. With its decorative cast-iron spandrels and pilasters complementing the recessed window bays, it was not an unattractive building, though the large expansions to the north side added in 1958 and 1962 made the county's house of justice appear lopsided and off-balance. Above the heavy bronze doors of the main entrance, a stone lintel depicted chained prisoners being set free by a judge, to the joy of an assembled crowd.

At 8:45 a.m. a green Cadillac pulled to the curb. Frank and Dorothy Smith stepped out, their every move and nuance noted by the clamoring reporters, photographers, and camera

Frank and Dorothy Smith's carefully orchestrated surrender to Sheriff Raymond Frank on January 31, 1977. The crime boss had dropped out of sight almost two weeks earlier, leading to speculation that he had fled to Mexico to avoid prosecution.

operators. But instead of going up the stairs to the bronze doors, the couple opted for the ground floor entrance, which led to the sheriff's office.

Frank Smith wore his dark brown leather coat, an orange shirt, and orange-and-brown checked pants; the usual comb-over and dimpled smirk were in place, his eyes hidden behind sunglasses. Her arm tightly hooked on his, Dorothy was whisper-thin in a stylish pantsuit, jauntily cocked chapeau, and large sunglasses. Quietly trailing the Smiths was their attorney, Paul T.

Holt, instantly identifiable in his trademark natty ensemble: electric-green suit, red tie, red socks. His nickname was "Red." The attorney was there to represent Smith as he turned himself in. Smith had been missing in action for ten days. The speculation concerning his whereabouts had intensified after the county grand jury indicted him on a charge of armed robbery and added to that a habitual criminal count.

A conviction for armed robbery would mark Smith's fourth felony conviction, one more than the minimum required by the state constitution to charge him as a habitual offender—which carried an automatic life sentence. Additionally, a person indicted on the charge could be held without bail for sixty days pending trial—an ironic dilemma for the former bail bond king in the capital city.

The reporters peppered the infamous couple with questions, desperately trying to get a statement from a man who had previously been one of the most reliable quote machines in the county, but Frank, zip-lipped mum, gave them nothing. Dorothy smiled as they marched forward. A photo of the couple as they stepped through the doors to the sheriff's office shows Dorothy leading Frank, like a mother taking a hesitant child to a doctor's appointment.

Carol Fowler captured the moment for the *Austin Citizen*. "The normally affable Smith, always ready with an easy grin and quick quip, didn't open his mouth, though his surrender had all the elements of an orchestrated press event," she wrote. "Both electronic press and newspaper reporters began arriving at the courthouse early today, tipped well in advance that the elusive Smith was turning himself in.[1]

Did Dorothy and Frank believe that making a dramatic production out of his surrender would improve his chance of getting the charges dropped or, in case of a trial, an acquittal? The Smiths did, in fact, seem to believe that they could handle Ronnie Earle, the new district attorney. Experienced attorneys, heavy connections, good luck, and cash infusions in the right places had worked in the past, so why not try to bluff their way through this time as well?

By staging his surrender for the media, appearing unbowed and unashamed, Frank wanted the public to see him as a big, important man subjected to a great injustice, targeted by a new, woefully inexperienced district attorney—a ruthlessly ambitious young politician who hoped to make a name for himself by nailing the mighty Frank Smith.

So far the year 1977 had not been good to Frank. Monday, January 3, the first day of business for the year, was swearing-in day at the courthouse. Frank was more than a little concerned about several of the new top officials. Frank Ivy, the new justice of the peace, was a booster for personal bonds and had a very unfavorable opinion of professional bondsmen. James McMurtry, county attorney, and Ronnie Earle, district attorney, were of the same mind.[2]

The departed county attorney, Ned Granger, had been a friend and ally of Frank Smith's, and everybody knew it, but it was not until Granger's last day in office that people began to realize how shamelessly he had employed his powers in office to help Smith: Granger had allowed Smith to settle ninety-seven forfeited misdemeanor bonds worth $70,000 for $7,627, or about ten cents on the dollar.[3] Although Granger had also allowed other bondsmen and attorneys (Paul Holt, for example) to slide on expensive forfeitures, the other favors showed just what an elected official can do for his real friends. At five p.m., December 31, 1976, Granger had filed a suit, with Travis County named as the plaintiff, against Ike and Jane Rabb's Salvage Pool, seeking $100,000 in damages. The suit was virtually identical to the suit filed by Frank Smith, except that it was backed by the authority and legal prowess of Travis County.

Reactions to Granger's parting gifts were sharply critical. From his city editor's desk at the *Statesman*, Ray Mariotti set the tone with an op-ed scorcher titled "Granger's Poor Legacy."[4] But Granger was gone, and so were his policies. In a public statement, new county attorney James McMurtry stated that his staff would be filing suit on forfeited bonds whenever it was practical to do so.

Granger's settlements with Frank Smith were set aside by a judge on January 4. The next day, the lawsuit filed by Granger against the Rabbs was considered in court and thrown out. The following Monday, Frank Smith's lawsuit against the Rabbs was tossed onto the same slag heap.[5]

Additional research on Smith's bonds turned up an additional $200,000 worth of forfeitures that had been ignored or written off. The decision on whether to pursue or settle the new batch of forfeitures was up to the district attorney, Ronnie Earle. Earle publicly stated that he wanted to collect on as many of Smith's forfeits as practically possible.[6]

As for Granger, the stench of guilt-by-association did not seem to bother him. The former county attorney said he was using Frank Smith's client list to solicit new customers for his private practice. Granger seemed to be flipping the bird at everybody on his way out the door.

Tressa Granger, Ned's dutiful daughter, agreed with that interpretation. "Of course," she said, with a loud chuckle, "it was Ned giving the world a big *F***you*." Tressa was sixteen years old when Ned lost his bid for district attorney, his last campaign for public office. She had worked on her father's campaigns going back to 1968.

When she was eight years old, Ned would drop her off at a discount store to pass out campaign pamphlets. "I'd stand there all day saying 'Will you vote for my daddy? Will you vote for my daddy?' He'd bring me lunch and then pick me up about five o'clock."

She recalled, "I grew up in the courthouse. I worked for my dad. When I skipped school, I didn't go to detention, I went to work. I would void hot checks at the courthouse, and I'd go riding with him at night, Daddy and Frank, when they were trying to find people who skipped bonds."

Ronnie Earle winning the district attorney race in 1976 was the last thing Tressa and her father expected.

"We were devastated when he lost the election," she said. "Totally surprised and devastated. He went off to Europe for a month to find himself and left me here alone. He came back with a new attitude." Tressa's relationship with officials and support staff at the courthouse continued through the years, including two and a half decades during which she owned a court reporting agency. In 2020 she was asked to comment on a sample of contemporary news stories regarding her father's forfeiture settlements and the lawsuit against the Rabbs. "Now we see what he had planned," she said. "I only wish I knew what he got in return."

Admirers of Ronnie Earle's long tenure as the county prosecutor may find it difficult to believe, but in the late 1970s, members of the courthouse establishment often underestimated the man with the Beatles haircut and crooked teeth. Even the courthouse good old boys who acknowledged Earle's keen intelligence and dedication to the law were still liable to cackle and drawl the following caveat: *But Ronnie Earle has never tried a case before a jury. Who wants a district attorney with no trial experience?* The outgoing district attorney, the cigar chomping Bob O. Smith, was a man of vast experience—in private practice, as county district attorney, and working with the state attorney general. Now the courthouse buzzed like a tin can packed with 999 cicadas: *Here we are, with one of the biggest criminal cases in recent memory, and the district attorney has never tried a single case in court.*

Long before Smith's case came to trial, however, Earle was diligently laboring to seal off all the exits for the alleged criminal mastermind, making moves that would overhaul the county bond system and make it a model for statewide reform, and 999 other things. But first things first: Earle was a member of the Travis County Bail Bond Board, and in mid-January the board voted to suspend Smith's license. It was only a two-day suspension, based on a technicality (Smith had not submitted a formal application for renewal but merely sent a letter stating his intention to renew it), though more serious infractions were heard by the board during the two-day suspension. Lt. Bobby Simpson, head of the Greater Austin Area Organized Crime Unit (OCU), submitted an affidavit to the board in which he presented convincing evidence that Smith's "moral reputation" in the community was "bad." Simpson was an authority on the scuzziest, most morally challenged actors of the Austin underworld, and his word carried a lot of weight. The suspension was made permanent.[7]

The heat was on. The Smiths were becoming more isolated every day. Many of the friends, supporters, and enablers who had happily advanced in Frank Smith's circles, helping him become rich and powerful, were now looking for a stealthy retreat. Alton Smithey, the sheriff of Hays County, was in some ways typical.[8] Smith bragged that his support was the reason Smithey won election to sheriff in 1976. Smithey's two-term predecessor, Bobby Kinser, had refused to allow Smith to write bonds in Hays County, but Smithey welcomed Smith's business, or at least he did until Smith's recent troubles. In an interview with Bill Cryer for the *Statesman*, Smithey lashed back at the troubled bondsman. "Everybody thinks that just because he's run his damn big mouth," he said. "He's the one who's put me on the spot, and I've had a belly full of it." Smith's unusual habit of writing checks to his underlings—arsonists, gunsels, and pliant sheriffs—ended up as evidence of guilt for both payer and payee in court.[9]

Dottie Ross, who ran the bail bond office and remained a Frank Smith partisan through thick and thin, mentioned highlights of Smith's efforts to get friendly sheriffs elected, including Smithey in Hays County, Wallace Riddell in Burnet County, and, of course, Raymond Frank in Travis County. They even got Willie Nelson to perform at an event for Raymond Frank, she said.

The Alton Smithey campaign was a lot of work for a "little, skinny, dumb" guy, she said. "He was the dumbest guy you ever saw in your life. So Frank hid him from everybody. He wouldn't let him talk to anybody; he wouldn't let him debate. He just kept him out of the limelight as much as possible." She laughed. "He was tall and skinny and always had a big old cowboy hat on," she continued. "But he was dumb! Frank thought that was the funniest thing he ever saw. So he groomed this man, and we made him sheriff. We got him elected, and that was a celebration, because we got the bonds. When people got in jail, he'd call us."

One of the worst bits of news for the Smiths stemmed from the arrest of a fourth suspect in the Salvage Pool robbery, Joseph Daniel "Red" Holt. He was a sixty-six-year-old ex-con with a criminal record that began with moonshine smuggling: transporting bootleg booze in a fast car and stashing it under his chicken coop between runs.[10] In the intervening years, Holt had been arrested for counterfeiting, armed robbery, and various other offenses. FBI agents had arrested Holt in Oklahoma City on January 13, 1977. He was being held pending extradition when, in a bizarre breach of protocol, Sheriff Frank flew to Oklahoma on his own, without consulting or notifying any other legal authorities. Many suspicious phone calls were made, including one in which the sheriff called Frank Smith, then put Red Holt on the phone for a while. Frank talked Holt into returning to Austin. Walking down the terminal at the Austin airport with his prisoner in tow, flashbulbs popping and TV camera lights glaring, the sheriff grinned broadly as he fielded reporters' questions. That night Holt was locked up, held on $250,000 bail for armed robbery, and the next morning, Sheriff Frank was called before the

The secret flight of Sheriff Raymond Frank (*left*) to Oklahoma City, where he convinced accused robber Red Holt (*right*) to return with him to Austin, met with the disapproval of DA Ronnie Earle, a federal grand jury, and the FBI. The reporter at far left is Victor Solis; Chief Deputy Jim Collier (*in hat*) stands at far right.

county grand jury, which demanded he explain his suspicious, unprofessional breach of precedent and protocol. The *Statesman* referred to the session as a "rump-chewing," but we can safely assume that the actual terms were less polite.[11]

Tuesday, January 25, in a meeting with Ronnie Earle and other officials in the DA's office, Holt agreed to testify against Frank Smith if the indictment against him was dropped. A surprise witness at the county grand jury the next afternoon, Holt took the stand at two p.m. His testimony must have been convincing, because at three p.m., Frank Smith was indicted for armed robbery and being a habitual offender. As usual, Bill Cryer was paying close attention. "Ronnie Earle," he wrote, "could barely conceal his joy at the return of the Smith indictment."[12]

Meanwhile, just four quick blocks away at the US courthouse on West Eighth Street, the federal grand jury was investigating possible corrupt ties between Sheriff Raymond Frank and Frank

Smith. As per the usual protocol, the hearings were closed to the public, including the media, though the list of witnesses was not difficult to uncover, and in contrast to the county grand jury, it was not illegal for witnesses to discuss their testimony in public.

Red Holt may have been the most important witness in town that day, but the proceedings at the art deco US courthouse heard an impressive parade of picaresque Austin personalities. First was Sam Houston Johnson, the younger brother of Lyndon Johnson and a friend of both Sheriff Frank and Frank Smith. Johnson's brilliance as a political insider was still generally acknowledged, but at this point his physical condition was frail, and the erudition of his brilliant mind had faded. Next up was Ned Granger, the former county attorney. John Pfluger was Smith's close friend and president of First State Bank of Pflugerville; he was an important witness because certain public officials who were friends of Frank Smith often obtained loans from First State Bank.[13] Pfluger was one of the handful of individuals that Frank Smith trusted implicitly, according to Letisha Taylor. Smith's business relationship with the bank started when Pfluger's father, also named John, was president of the bank. The younger Pfluger, Taylor said, was "one of the best friends I ever had. He was a good man."

In addition to being friends with one or both the Two Franks, some of the grand jury witnesses had ties with the Austin underworld that stretched back more than a decade and included numerous individuals who had been associated with the Overton Gang, which was active in the 1960s. Early in the decade a loose syndicate of bank burglars, pimps, drug dealers, and professional gamblers had made Austin its home base but had largely concentrated its criminal activity in other areas. The titular leader of the group was James Timothy "Timmy" Overton, an ex-UT football star. The gang faded out after some of the main figures, including Timmy Overton, were convicted and sentenced in a 1968 federal bank burglary conspiracy trial. By that time several other prominent members of the gang were already serving prison sentences.[14] Overton was released on parole in 1972; two months later he was shot to death in Dallas, along with his girlfriend, by a member of the same circle of Austin underworld figures. By 1972 most of Overton's former criminal cohorts who were still involved in illegal activities were being watched by authorities in connection with a wider criminal network generally referred to as the Dixie Mafia, known to be active not only in Texas but also in several other states, particularly in the Deep South.[15]

Another witness at the federal hearing was Robyn Schnautz, the young blonde widow of ex-Overton Gang member Travis Schnautz. The couple owned a downtown massage parlor called D.W. Rubb. After Travis was shotgunned to death there back in August 1976, interest ratcheted up around the activities of the former cohorts of Timmy Overton. Police initially feared that Travis's murder might be related to internecine squabbles between the alumni, but investigators zeroed in on a stronger suspect—Robyn's boyfriend, too young to have been a member of the Overton club—but he was released due to lack of evidence.

On February 5, 1976, an article in the *Statesman* titled "Junkyard Suspects May Be in State Ring" cited a new DPS bulletin that reported that Frank Smith, along with the four "alleged accomplices" in the Salvage Pool robbery, plus eight other men, were "suspected members of a larger ring of bandits that holds up 'gamblers and people connected with organized crime.'" The bulletin included the names of nine other ex-cons, the majority of whom were known to be former members of the Overton Gang.

Travis Schnautz had been under the eye of federal authorities for at least two decades by the time of his sensational demise. Perhaps more important to the history of Austin's cultural identity, Travis and Robyn, during happier times, had been a symbolic link between Austin's burgeoning outlaw country music scene and Austin's regular outlaws, the ones who trafficked in felonies, not fiddles, though it was sometimes hard to tell the difference between the former and the latter.

Travis and Robyn had purchased their massage parlor in 1975 with financial assistance from outlaw country star Willie Nelson. According to employees, Willie was a regular visitor at D.W. Rubb, where, it was said, patrons could gratify a wide variety of illicit desires not limited to sex and drugs. Travis, Robyn, and Willie had been seen together at Armadillo World Headquarters, the beloved music hall famed for bringing rednecks from the cedar breaks in the hills down to Austin where they mixed with longhaired hippies and radicals, communing together over country music, cold beer, and cheap Mexican weed.

Strongly suspected by cops and crooks alike as the person who had hired her boyfriend to kill her husband, Robyn acquired the sobriquet "Black Widow." Chester Schutz, one of the surviving convicted bank burglars of the Overton Gang, was still embedded with Austin's alt-society of crime and vice. Schutz elbowed the boyfriend aside and became Robyn's consort. Chester was also reputed to be the muscle for Frank Smith.

Frank Smith became scarce after Red Holt's arrest. Bill Cryer left a message on Frank's answering machine on January 19. Two days later, an uncharacteristically long delay, Smith finally returned his call, saying, "I'm going to take a vacation to let my head clear and try to figure out what all of this is about." Regarding Aymon Armstrong, Smith said, "I don't know him, I've never seen him before, I've never heard of him before." Smith refused to tell Cryer where he was going, only that he was "going south" and would be out of town for "a couple of weeks of fishing."[16]

And then Frank dropped completely out of sight. Or so it seemed. Dorothy Smith gave statements that backed up Frank's responses to Cryer, but they were almost comically vague. He was going fishing, she said, maybe in Mexico.[17] In reality, Frank was staying in a motel on North I-35 at St. John's Avenue. Dottie Ross, his bond office assistant, was then living at Frank's house on St. John's. Dottie took his calls and delivered meals from his favorite eating places. She took him Mexican dinners from El Patio, a hole-in-the-wall Tex-Mex cafe on the north end of the university Drag, where the salsa was served with crackers instead of chips. Other favorites were the NightHawk, a red-vinyl-booth steakhouse owned by Harry Akin, a much-respected civic leader and former Austin mayor, and Piccadilly Cafeteria, a buffet place at Capital Plaza shopping center, just a short hop down the interstate.

During Frank's brief time out of the public eye, he signed over deeds for more than one hundred acres of real estate valued at $200,000 to Dorothy's name. With the help of good friend John Pfluger at the First State Bank of Pflugerville, Dorothy secured a $50,000 loan.

Speculation as to Smith's whereabouts intensified after the indictment came down on Thursday, January 27, the day after Red Holt's testimony. Over the weekend the US attorney filed a complaint with the federal magistrate in Austin, a move that would authorize the FBI to join the search the following Monday.[18] On Sunday, Dorothy informed the authorities that Frank was on his way back to town and would surrender that evening. He had been out of pocket, fishing, she said, and only just learned of the indictments. Later that day she gave an update, saying that Frank had had "car trouble," which would delay his arrival, but that he would surrender early the next morning. That same night reporters all over Austin received phone calls from the publicity-savvy couple: be at the courthouse Monday morning for the spectacle of Frank Smith surrendering to Sheriff Raymond Frank. Dorothy made some of the calls; the prodigal fisherman made the others.[19]

At the request of Frank Smith's attorney, Paul Holt, a hearing on bail convened Wednesday, February 2, Judge Mace Thurman presiding. Earle and First Assistant District Attorney Phil

Nelson had a lot riding on the hearing. Earle wanted Smith held without bail. In the case of a habitual offender, bail could be denied, pending a trial in sixty days, if the state could provide "evidence substantially showing the guilt of the accused," as specified by Article I, Sec. 11-a of the state constitution.[20]

Phil Nelson had been a prosecutor in the DA's office for years. Behind his quiet, understated manner was a lawyer with keen intuition, razor-sharp skills, and a commanding knowledge of the law. Interestingly, Nelson had been one of the prosecutors who left the DA's office for private practice after Ronnie Earle was elected. One of Ronnie's most important moves early on was to convince Nelson to come back after only the briefest chance to pursue a private law practice. "I think he just really missed being a prosecutor," said Bill Cryer, who first met Nelson in the mid-1960s while covering the courthouse beat. "I think he just found private practice was too boring for him." In any event, after joining Earle's team, Nelson dove into the work as if he realized he had returned to the job he was born to do.

Isaac Rabb was the first of three state witnesses to testify at the bail hearing on Wednesday. Rabb was impressive on the witness stand, an outdoorsman and working man by appearance, his Louisiana upbringing evidenced by the accent and cadences of his speech, which was marked by unaffected, bare-bones declarative statements, plus occasional reminders that he was college educated and intelligent. To Ronnie Earle's question about the events of Friday, December 3, 1976, Rabb testified:

> At six p.m. I was standing at a table in our office counting cash to make a deposit. I looked up over my left shoulder. There appeared inside the office a man wearing a monster mask, a jumpsuit and carrying a gun. I immediately reacted and jumped across the room to my 20-gauge shotgun.[21]

Ike Rabb fired two fatal shotgun rounds at McKnight, left his pocket pistol with wrecker driver Luther New to guard the dying bandit, and ran outside to shoot at the other two masked robbers, who were also firing at him. Then came a moment of terrible panic.

I thought of my youngest daughter being in the house. I ran toward the house. I saw a man standing behind some bushes. I fired again and he ran off. My daughter actually wasn't there, but at the time I was afraid she'd been kidnapped. I forgot that she had gone to a friend's birthday party.

On cross-examination, attorney Paul Holt asked Rabb why Smith had paid such a large sum in cash. "I requested it," answered Rabb. "I felt it would be a harassment. I had lots of problems with Mr. Smith." Later lawyer Holt asked Rabb if he had seen Frank Smith during the actual robbery. Rabb said no.

Joseph Daniel "Red" Holt took the stand late that afternoon, absent the fedora that went so well with his wide-lapeled suede coat. He was balding, with longish, curly, red-and-gray hair artfully combed on the back and sides. He was short, round-shouldered, and a bit comical looking. To Phil Nelson's question regarding the plea bargain with the prosecutor to which he had agreed, Holt replied in a gravelly voice and a red-dirt country accent, "I was previously indicted, then the charges were dismissed." Nelson: "You made an agreement with the district attorney for your testimony?" Holt: "Yes, sir."

The reason for his trip to Austin to see Frank Smith? "I came down to see if he would invest in copper pictures of Jesus Christ and an Indian chief," Holt replied. "He said he would talk about it. I called him about a week before that to see if he'd be interested." Red was looking for an investment of $40,000, but soon after he arrived in Austin, Frank Smith proposed an alternate agenda for the weekend.

Driving his white 1966 Oldsmobile, Holt arrived in Austin Thursday, December 2, and booked a room at the E-Z Travel Motor Hotel on I-35 on the far northern edge of town. Why that particular motel? "It was a $9.95 price up there." Smith came to the motel. They had a few drinks, then went downtown to visit his bail bond office. Friday morning they went to Smith's salvage yard, and Smith made his first pitch for the heist.

> RED HOLT: We sat out there talking and . . . Chester Schutz came out. We bulled a little . . . and then Chester left. He said there was a salvage dealer and he was going to pay him $15,000 . . . and he wanted us to rob it. Me and somebody else. I told him I didn't know. I didn't care about it. He said it would be a piece of cake. He wanted a third of it.
>
> NELSON: Did you agree to participate in this robbery?
>
> RED HOLT: No, sir.

Leaving Pflugerville, the pair drove south to have a look at the site of the proposed robbery. Holt took note of the narrow blacktop road connecting the Austin Salvage Pool to Dalton Lane.

> RED HOLT: He drove by it and said that's it. We drove back by it again. I told him it looked pretty raunchy to me . . . rough to get in.
>
> NELSON: A rough place to pull a robbery?
>
> RED HOLT: Yes, sir. He said he had some boys coming down from Fort Worth to take care of it. He said one of them was McKnight. . . . I knew him from Leavenworth. I also met Frank Smith there.

Joseph Daniel "Red" Holt (*left*) enjoyed a long and varied career in crime, from smuggling bootleg whiskey in Oklahoma to counterfeiting, armed robbery, and fraud. Note in this photo that he is wearing a coat borrowed from Deputy Jim Collier (who's seen wearing it in the photo of Holt's arrival from Oklahoma).

If Holt's version of the robbery was a heist film, it wouldn't be an American production but a film noir by a French New Wave director from the late 1950s, perhaps Jean-Pierre Melville. At times, whenever the criminals testified about their movements, various old landmarks crop up in the narrative, offering glimpses of Austin as it was in the last quarter of the twentieth century. When Holt mentioned a dinner meeting at "the Mexican place," he was referring to La Tapatia, which was one of the classier Tex-Mex restaurants on Sixth Street in East Austin, a predominantly

Hispanic neighborhood that by the 2020s was being developed and gentrified beyond recognition.

About one o'clock I met Chester at the Mexican place. We went there. We had dinner. Frank said he had some business to take care of. Chester let me off at the motel. Frank said he would be there about three or three-thirty. Chester and I drove around a while and drank beer. It was about three when we got back to the motel. About 3:30 at the motel he came in with McKnight. . . . He showed us a zipper bag, a money bag, and said it was $15,000.

He said he had to get on out there. He said they would be tight, drunk, there won't be any trouble, but if there is, just waste 'em. He said to be there right at six o'clock.

McKnight and I drank some beer and scotch. About 4:30 we went to Pancake House and had lunch. At about quarter to six he said he would go get his partner. We left. He introduced me to his partner [Aymon Armstrong].

We drove by the place and we seen Smith's car was still there. McKnight's partner was driving. I was in the back seat, McKnight in the front seat.

Frank was still there. We held up . . . put on coveralls, ski mask and a pair of gloves. The other two had rubber masks. . . .

I had a pistol under the seat. Frank Smith came out and stopped. . . . He got in his car. . . . We started in driving toward the . . . wrecking yard. Frank stopped. He said there was right at $27,000 in there and they've been drinking. It'll be a piece of cake. . . .

McKnight got out. . . . He got in the wrecker with the boys. He got into the wrecker. We turned around. The wrecker headed up to the office and stopped when it was around . . . 40 feet from the office. McKnight got out and went in. His partner got out and went inside the office. About then I heard a shot, then two more shots . . . two

pistol shots and one shotgun shot. The pistol shot first.
His partner came running out and I asked what's the
matter? He said all hell broke loose.

A man came out and shot twice at me. I shot twice in
the air and then I ran, too. I took off the coveralls and
threw the pistol away. I ran out to west. A car pulled out.
I hid by a church and waited until there were no cars. I
went onto the highway. I went to a U-tot-em and called
Frank to come and get me.

He said OK. He came out. I told him all hell broke
loose and we were put in a trap. Then he said No, he was
sorry things happened that way, but he didn't put us in
a trap. We had some Scotch and headed toward town.

We went to the bonding office and then went to the
Chinese place. At the Chinese place I met a heavyset guy
by the name of Doc. A blond guy.

The "Chinese place" where Smith and Holt dined was Three
Sisters, a small Chinese cafe on Burnet Road, one of the few Chinese restaurants in Austin in 1977.

Frank said he was sorry that it happened like that. He
said he didn't send us into a trap. Frank took me back to
the motel.

I saw him the next day about 9:30. We went to Piccadilly Cafeteria. We went by the bonding office. He gave
me a $300 check for expenses. He said not to stop in
Wichita Falls to look for a colored girl. I went and cashed
the check. The check was in my name. Then I left.

Nelson passed the witness. Smith's attorney, Paul "Red" Holt,
began his cross-examination of witness Joseph Daniel "Red"
Holt by asking again about the purpose of his trip to Austin.
The "picture deal," as Holt referred to it, was "the only reason
for this trip," he said.

There were several questions about Red Holt's criminal history. A conviction for possession of counterfeit money was the reason he had taken up housekeeping at Leavenworth.[22] The attorney asked Holt how many times he had been arrested. "I used to bootleg," which led to "about fifty arrests," he answered, adding, "I used to get arrested for whiskey every two or three days." Two other specific charges were the burglary of a service station in 1936 and "transporting a pistol when I was bootlegging."

Attorney Holt wanted more details about the robbery. He asked the Oklahoman when he made up his mind to participate in the heist.

> Chester took me back to the motel. Met McKnight at the motel. Mr. Smith met us about 3:30. I was drinking ... beer and Scotch. Couple of drinks. Then we went to the Pancake House. McKnight came with Mr. Smith. He initiated the conversation. He said he had to get on out there. I told him I would stay in the car. That's when I said I would go.[23]

Ronnie Earle's other star witness was John Calvin Bailey, forty-three, a slender, one-legged junkie poet with a record of convictions going back to 1955. An admitted heroin addict ("off and on, for twenty-eight years," he said) who dressed like a character: hair slicked back, full beard, black-framed glasses, shirt collar spread wide, pressed slacks, and black-and-white wingtips—Stacey Adams, the expensive footwear of choice for gangsters, pimps, and thieves. If Bailey had a profession aside from poetry and the gigs he performed for Frank Smith, it was shoplifting. In fact, it was shoplifting that precipitated his agreement to testify. The district attorney's office had agreed to drop shoplifting charges against Bailey in exchange for his "truthful testimony." Bailey had confessed to being one of three men that Smith had hired to burn down the Austin Salvage Pool on October 18, 1976, and he had other areas of knowledge about Smith's criminality as well.

On direct examination by Phil Nelson, Bailey soon demonstrated his value as a witness for the state. Asked if he had had a "conversation with Smith" regarding the robbery at the Austin Salvage Pool, Bailey answered, "He just discussed with me that it was a blowed deal, the people who had done it had messed it up completely."

> I know there was a mention that people from Fort Worth had blowed the deal. He had left the money off at Rabb's place and he informed the people to go get it. . . . Smith said he wanted to see him hurt financially and that he wanted him to suffer some mental anguish.

Like Red Holt, Bailey spoke in the hardboiled lingo of the streets—"a blowed deal"—but he was obviously an emissary from that world who loved language and loved to talk.

A *Statesman* headline writer paid tribute to Bailey's way with words the following day: "Witness: Smith Planned Robbery to Cause 'Anguish.'"[24] The article excerpted key sections of exchanges between witnesses and attorneys, including the moment when attorney Holt asked hapless arsonist Bailey, point blank, "Why would Smith like you?"

> BAILEY: Because he trusted me.
> PAUL HOLT: Why you?
> BAILEY: Because he knew . . . he couldn't find anybody to do it and I would do it. With this other matter . . . he trusted me enough to run his business down to me because he knew what my business was. He knew I could be trusted to take care of a matter he couldn't do himself. . . .
> He asked me to burn Mr. Rabb's junkyard down for him. I can't remember the date.

Smith had told Bailey he wanted the office trailer destroyed along with seventy of the newer wrecks on the lot. Smith even instructed Bailey on what kind of fuel to use to ignite the blaze. Under redirect by Nelson, additional details were revealed, such as the names of Bailey's accomplices.[25]

NELSON: Who helped you?

BAILEY: Two partners, William Ashabranner and Santiago "Jimbo" Soto. We were to be paid $1,500. We weren't paid the full amount. He gave me a $600 check on what he wrote for bond jumping or something like that . . . work for bond jumping. . . .

I went to his bank. The teller shorted me $100. I had to come back.[26]

Frank Smith's unusual habit of paying for criminal acts by check had come back to bite him again; the bank teller felt bad about short-changing Bailey, which helped imprint the encounter on her memory.

Three witnesses were called by Smith to testify in support of his plea for a reasonable bail. At least two of them had done business at Smith's wrecking yard. All three gave mildly positive answers to questions about Smith being released on bail, including the lukewarm responses of a former deputy sheriff. Attorney Holt asked the witness about the time in 1967 when Smith was free on bail between courtroom appearances.

PAUL HOLT: Did he ever fail to show up?

WITNESS: No, sir. He always did what he said he would do. He always was himself.

PAUL HOLT: Can you think of a reason that Mr. Smith should be denied bond?

WITNESS: I don't know of anything.

After the state rested its case, Ron Littlepage observed a "pained look" on Judge Thurman's face as he announced his decision. "As I read Section 11a, bond may be denied by court," he said. Due to the "extreme seriousness of the offense charged—proved in accordance with the article, I believe for that reason I'm going to deny bond."

Attorney Holt gave notice that Smith would appeal the judge's ruling, the hearing was adjourned, and the prisoner was escorted from the courtroom to his cell on the sixth floor of the courthouse.

Ron Littlepage incorporated his notes from the bail hearing into a feature for the *Austin Citizen* titled "The Full Shootout Story." The layout emulated a 1950s black-and-white film noir, with a dramatic photo of the chicken coop office, close-up pictures of firearms on a desk, and a six-photo box titled "Cast of Characters," featuring Ike Rabb, Ronnie Earle, Judge Mace Thurman, Red Holt, Aymon Armstrong, and Willie McKnight. Captions gave brief explanations of the role of each respective actor in the drama.

Above the lead paragraph was a photo of Red Holt, pulling the brim of his fedora down in front of his face, but not so low as to hide his grin.[27]

In the *Statesman* Bill Cryer took a satirical approach. "Smith Mastermind? Salvage Heist Badly Bungled" shoots bullets of absurdity from the first line: "If the legend of Frank H. Smith is believed and he is a mastermind of crime, then testimony last week of his role in the aborted armed robbery of the Austin Salvage Pool casts doubt on the state of the criminal art in Travis County."

"The case is so bizarre, its characters so overdrawn, that at times it has seemed that someone is following the text of a satire on the criminal mentality," Cryer continued. "It would be amusing if the life of one man had not been forfeited in the attempted robbery and the lives and welfare of a family jeopardized in the process."[28]

On February 9 the county grand jury indicted Frank Smith for arson in the October fire at the Salvage Pool.[29] Smith launched a counteroffensive from his jail cell, against not just Ronnie Earle but also a vaguely described "conspiracy of defense attorneys" and the jailers who supervised his imprisonment. In the beginning Smith had refused to put on his jail uniform, commonly referred to as "county whites." Smith sat in his cell in his underwear until the sheriff relented and ordered Smith's jeans and shirts returned to him. Media representatives besieged Sheriff Frank to grant them interviews with the infamous prisoner, but they were denied. The sheriff gave a variety of reasons: because Smith did not have an attorney of record, because he wouldn't put on his jail whites, or because of security concerns.

The last excuse did have merit. Ronnie Earle had notified Sheriff Frank that an informant had contacted him with the following warning: "The word in jail is there are three 'hit' men in Fort Worth out to get Smith."[30]

Smith fired off vitriolic letters, complaining to the sheriff about the conditions of his confinement and sending ferocious missives directly to specific jailers. On the evening of February 11, Officer Thompson sent a message his superior, Captain Falin, about a tense situation at the jail.

> At 1930 hrs. Mrs. Smith stated that last football season, the sheriff, Frank Smith and Smith's son went to Houston to an Oilers' game. At the hotel the sheriff shacked up with a woman in [Mrs. Smith's] son's presence. Mrs. Smith said she was going to call Mrs. Frank tonight (2-11-77) and inform her of the incident. Mrs. Smith stated she was going to inform the press of the incident and was going to take everybody down with them.[31]

The memo, the letter from Earle about the death threat, and many other related items were filed in a manila folder in the sheriff's office marked "Frank Smith." Smith's sprawling long-hand letters complained about jail restrictions, threatened retaliation, nursed personal grudges, and offered constructive criticism on housekeeping at the jail. Several documents attest to the fact that Smith received special treatment. For the average prisoner, making a phone call was a hassle, but not for Frank; he could use the pay phone right outside his cell. After a brief media embargo during Smith's first week in jail, his access to the media was restored, along with his wardrobe. On the first day he was allowed to speak to reporters, Smith scheduled a press conference during his allotted fifteen minutes of visiting time. The jailors allowed the event to stretch on past an hour.

During the press conference Smith read from a prepared statement in which he maintained his innocence and complained that being "denied the right to talk to the press . . . violated my right of free speech and also freedom of the press—two things every American should enjoy." In answer to the indictments against him, Smith had his own indictments for the district attorney. "In order to deny my bail and my right to get out and investigate the true facts . . . the district attorney brought in off the streets a known heroin addict and drug salesman. . . . What has happened to the presumption of innocence in this country?"[32]

He was a victim of Ronnie Earle's political ambition, he said, "just because Ronnie Earl wants to be attorney general or governor." Over the coming weeks Smith would repeat his political attacks again and again, honing his insults and incorporating crude vulgarities. Political ambitions? If only Smith had known the great satisfaction Ronnie Earle derived from serving Travis County as its chief law enforcer.

On February 6, 1977, Bill Cryer wrote that a letter written by Smith in his cell had been "discovered" that included the following requests: "Need these things. . . . above all, get Cryer up. Get Sutton up. Also call Carol Fowler. Call KTBC. Call Channel

36. Want all up here." The letter, which apparently had been "leaked" to the press by someone in the jail or sheriff's office, is typical of the notes to be found in the Frank Smith file in the sheriff's office, documenting the ongoing symbiotic relationship between Smith and the media.

The letter obtained by Cryer, presumably written to Smith's wife, Dorothy, included two additional requests: "Write me a note and tell me what happened to the bald head col—also want Richard Goodman and Levi Isaack." The "bald head colonel" was a pet name for Raymond Frank; Goodman and Isaack were partners in a public relations firm who had done work for Smith's bail bond agency and also for political campaigns that Smith had been involved in.[33]

Smith's trial for armed robbery was scheduled for March 28, but a continuance was granted after Smith and his lead defense attorney, William "Wild Bill" Dunnam of Waco, hired an additional attorney, state representative Craig Washington of Houston.[34] The defense's foremost reason for hiring an additional attorney was its desire to delay the trial by employing a tactic called "legislative continuance." If a legislator is hired for a trial before the trial date is set, a postponement of thirty days after the legislative session is automatically granted upon notice to the court. In 1977 the regular session would be followed by a special session, which pushed the date even further. The trial date was reset for July 11.

The specific choice of Representative Washington made the move more interesting. Washington had recently waded into the debate over the reinstatement of the death penalty in Texas, after a thirteen-year hiatus, with guns figuratively blazing. This being Texas, some crazy ideas were being tossed around. A federal judge from Dallas jumped into the fray, ruling that executions could be televised. Two death row inmates promptly volunteered themselves for the honor. Attorney John Hill said he would appeal. "There are some things we just don't do," said Hill. "These people are human beings."[35]

Representative Washington, a criminal defense attorney, went even further, saying that capital punishment was "murder by the state," and that "until we can create life, we don't have the right to take it. We're not God." Before he made those statements, Washington had been chair of the Criminal Jurisprudence Committee; afterward, House Speaker Bill Clayton informed Washington that he no longer had that honor.

Washington was still chairman of the Black Legislative Caucus, however. He was a tall, good-looking, well-dressed, well-spoken African American, and he looked good on television. Those factors, taken together, help explain why Frank Smith, whose attitudes on race had a lot to do with his upbringing in segregated Waco, chose to hire a Black legislator/lawyer. Bill Cryer remembered Washington as "a brilliant, if unconventional politician. . . . He was a joy to cover as a newspaperman because he was always quotable with an engaging sense of the absurdity of being an intellectual Black male engaged in the not-so-intellectual roil of the Texas Legislature." Washington's admirers also included Ronnie and Twila Earle.

For someone who seemed to get what he wanted most of the time, Frank Smith complained an awful lot. On May 3 he sent his jailers a rambling letter complaining about dirt and roaches in the jail. The letter was enclosed in a Frank Smith & Sons Bail Bonds envelope bearing the company motto: "LET US HELP YOU OUT." The tone was polite and pleasant, but three weeks later Smith was raging again. One of the targets of his ire was chief jailer Craig Campbell, as attested in one of the more memorable sections of a missive from May 3, 1977.[36]

> You had no damn business calling me down there to that office to chew my ass out—I was up here minding my

own business bothering no one—the subject you discussed I knew nothing about at the time. If I'd been
directing getting anything to me in this jail you would
have been the last person I would have ever ask. I'd eat
shit before I'd ask you for anything.

That same day Campbell reminded Smith in a message that
he must comply with the rules and regulations, gently chastising
him for "verbal or physical abuse" against the officers of the jail.
"If you persist in creating a disturbance or trying to incite other
inmates to do such, we will be forced to take some action." The
tone of the message seems inexplicably wimpy, especially in light
of language such as, "We have tried to be fair with you. We ask
that you be fair with us."[37]

Sheriff Frank sent a letter to Smith the same day. Again, the
tone was both threatening and pleading. "All of us, for several
months now, have bent over backwards trying to make life as
pleasant as possible for you," he wrote. "One thing I am asking
you to do is cease immediately the violence that you are attempting in the jail. We will not tolerate it under any circumstances.
. . . Please do not make a threat to me."[38]

So it went, with the loudest mouth in Texas *blah-blah-blahing*
from his nine-by-twelve cell on the sixth floor, striving to make it
to page one and the top of the news hour, railing against the system, fighting against his jailers. Smith's attorneys went to court
to argue for bail repeatedly—at least five times—to no avail. Protesting the jail policy of sharing razors, Frank grew a beard. The
defendant who'd stalled his trial by using legislative delays filed
a motion protesting the denial of his right to a speedy trial. The
grand jury remained in session, using its subpoena power to give
Austin's graying thugs a reason to get out of bed before noon.
There were always new controversies swirling around Sheriff
Frank—many, if not all, related to Frank Smith.

THE TRIAL

I hope it can never be said that a jury in Gillespie
County can deprive a man of his family and his
liberty on the word of a dope addict.

—DEFENSE ATTORNEY PAT DOOLEY

The trial of Frank Smith, originally set for March in 147th District Court in Austin, was bumped down the calendar twice, eventually landing on September 19, 1977, in a new venue, the 216th District Court in Fredericksburg, seat of Gillespie County. During the last weeks of his seven months in jail, Frank had lashed out against Ronnie Earle and Judge Mace Thurman in the media with insults, innuendo, conspiracy theories, and scatological outbursts.

Dottie Ross, who had managed Frank Smith's bail bond office and remained a staunch Frank Smith loyalist, told Ron Littlepage that her employer was angry at Judge Thurman for continuously denying Smith's pleas for bail. "She said he is trying to organize picketing of Thurman's house," Littlepage wrote, adding that Ross said the protest "would make it clear that Smith is being held in jail on the word of two ex-cons, Holt and Bailey—a situation she called extremely 'unfair.'"[1]

In an interview in 2009 Dottie Ross said she still believed that Frank Smith had been treated unfairly. "I just don't actually think they had a real fair trial," she said. "I am not a believer in turning two or three people out who are real low-lifes to get [convict] one." Not that she believed he was innocent. Asked if Frank hired Bailey to burn down the Austin Salvage Pool, she said, "I never did know if he did that for sure or not. If I had to bet money on it, I would bet that he did." Did she think that Frank was guilty of committing the crimes he was accused of? "I think so."

The change of venue originated with a motion filed by Wild Bill Dunnam. He argued that the publicity overload in Travis County would make it impossible for his client to obtain a fair and impartial trial. At the hearing on the motion, First Assistant DA Phil Nelson agreed that there had been "a substantial amount of publicity" and that the state had no objection to the motion. Thurman granted the motion—which pleased Frank and his attorneys—and promptly transferred the trial to the 216th District Court in Fredericksburg, Gillespie County—which did not please them a bit.

Located eighty-one miles west of Austin, deep in the Hill Country, in 1977 Fredericksburg was a small town of fewer than six thousand, settled by German immigrants in the 1840s. "Fritztown," as it was often called, was a farm and ranch community where the descendants of the original homesteaders often spoke German in public and at home. Among the generation who grew up during the Depression and World War II, German was their first language; English was learned at school. High school football, the county fair and rodeo, Christian religious holidays, and parades were major red calendar events, and the pace of life picked up considerably when deer hunting season began every fall. Austin and San Antonio were the nearest urban centers, each over an hour's drive away. In the days before twenty-four-hour news and the profusion of cable TV—long before the internet—the geographic distance gave towns like Fredericksburg a sense of being outposts, of separateness.

Fredericksburg and the nearby towns of Stonewall and Johnson City enjoyed a fleeting moment in the spotlight during the 1960s, after Lyndon B. Johnson, who grew up in this corner of the Texas Hill Country, became president. Media representatives, followed closely by weekend tourists, descended on the Hill Country, marveling at its quaintness and quietude. Fredericksburg, with its stolid little storefronts, churches, and the steamboat-shaped Nimitz Hotel, childhood home of the great Admiral Chester Nimitz, was placed in the National Register of Historic Places in Texas in 1970. Today, tourists and expats continue to be drawn there by its remoteness, quirkiness, and the beauty of the surrounding countryside—not to mention the profusion of wineries in the region.[2]

But back in the late 1970s Fritztown folks were not accustomed to characters like Frank Smith, and it is difficult to imagine they would have felt much sympathy for his legal dilemmas. Considering the fact that Judge Thurman was receiving death threats when the case was in his court, we might presume that he had banged his last gavel on it with a sigh of relief and a guttural *Auf Wiedersehen*.

Death threats became a fact of life among people associated with the prosecution of Frank Smith. "There were contracts out on me," said Ike Rabb. "We had police protection for quite a while." Denise Ormand remembers her father sitting up nights next to the bedroom window with his shotgun.

The threatening phone calls, dark rumors, and messages also focused on Ronnie Earle and his family, according to Twila Earle. Once his divorce was finalized in March 1977, the web of terroristic intimidation spread even wider. Earle had become romantically involved with his former administrative assistant, Twila Hugley, a relationship that led to marriage in 1978 and lasted until Earle's death in 2020. Today, Twila Earle is still haunted by the campaign of death threats, vicious gossip, and other forms of intimidation she experienced during the years of Frank Smith.

"Ronnie and I both had children, and it was scary," she said in an interview for this book. "Frank's animosity was wide and it was deep, and he never forgave or forgot. He seemed to rejoice in inflicting loss and inspiring fear, misery, and dread.

"The great blessing for me out of all that was a lesson I learned from a personal security trainer during the worst of Smith's death threats," she said. "It helped me deal with his never-ending rage and hostility and the unresolved threat that lingered until his death, as well as other threats from other people in later years. My trainer told me, 'When someone is threatening to harm you, if they are serious, there is a limit to what you can do about it. So you take all reasonable steps and then *stop*. Don't let anyone take your quality of life with a threat.'"

Stories about Frank Smith's enemies being murdered, beaten, or threatened with murder had circulated for years. *Statesman* reporter Bill Cryer had notebooks full of them, some of them so dark they occasionally slipped out of the notebook and crept into his nightmares. Over several weeks in the hot and muggy late spring of 1977, Cryer interviewed the haunted and tearful mother of Jennifer Barton, an East Eleventh Street sex worker who had, for a time, been Smith's lover—until she dropped out of sight. Doggedly tracing the story through street contacts, cops, junkies, and relatives (including Barton's mother), Cryer found the weight of evidence strongly supported the story that Smith had her killed.[3]

One of Cryer's sources of inside information was a Hispanic private detective named R. G. Lopez. The stories were not always reliable, but they were always interesting. The most interesting story of all began to develop in the sweltering summer months leading up to the trial, and it featured Lopez himself as a contract killer for Frank Smith.

"Frank hired the private detective R. G. Lopez to put a hit on John Calvin Bailey," Cryer said. "R. G. Lopez used to work for Frank. He would run down bail jumpers for Frank and they were close."[4]

John Calvin Bailey and Red Holt were the two indispensable witnesses for the prosecution. Under the law Red Holt was a criminal accomplice, and therefore his testimony had to be corroborated by another witness. Absent Bailey, the prosecution's case was a house of cards in a hurricane.

R. G. Lopez was famous in Austin. Short and round, wearing a pinstripe suit with cocked fedora and mustache, he fit the general description of the nameless fictional detective in Dashiell Hammett's Continental Op stories, and, like Sam Spade, the detective in Hammett's great novel *The Maltese Falcon*, he had a reputation as a person with a flexible moral compass, which could be advantageous in his line of work.

Lopez had a plush office in the historic Littlefield Building, the great-granddaddy of Austin high-rises, where sexily attired females did his bidding. He drove a Cadillac with an arsenal of guns in the trunk. His praises were sung in a Mexican corrido written by conjunto legend Johnny Degollado.[5] When a briefcase belonging to Willie Nelson's manager mysteriously disappeared backstage during a gig, Willie hired Lopez to recover it. Lopez told the *Statesman* that he was authorized to spend "up to $1,000 a day to pay for information that will help me locate the briefcase. No questions asked."[6]

"R. G. was also an informant for the FBI at the time," said Cryer. "So we started meeting every Saturday morning at Pease Park by the swing sets, and he would tell me everything that Frank had told him up at the county jail. I had to promise him that I would not publish the story until the FBI was ready to file the charges."

The plotting began on June 13. One of Smith's employees gave Lopez a message that Smith wanted to see him. Lopez went to visit him. Smith told the detective he wanted him to find Bailey and get a deposition from him. Lopez sensed some ambiguity in the request. Describing that first meeting, he told Cryer that Smith was "talking in whispers and writing down most of the conversation." Then he asked Lopez if he had a business card on him, knowing full well that a self-promoter like him would

R. G. Lopez cultivated the popular image of a private eye and never seemed to lack for work, legitimate and otherwise. His secret meetings with Bill Cryer in the summer of 1977 were the stuff of a pulp fiction novel.

never be without one. "When I handed it to him," Lopez said, "he turned it over and wrote 'JCB . . . $5,000,'" then "slowly drew an 'X'" through Bailey's initials, whispering, "Forever and ever." Smith's intent was clear.

Lopez went to Lt. Bobby Simpson, head of the Organized Crime Unit, and informed him of the approach from Smith. Simpson called FBI Agent Bob Hoglund, who received permission from the US Attorney for Lopez to wear a wire. Lopez wore the wire to subsequent visits, despite how nervous it made him feel, betraying the confidence of a fellow character whose piercing stare had been known to disintegrate lesser souls.

Smith wanted Bailey killed by overdose, a concept he communicated through pantomime gestures and phrases written on a legal pad. The price for the murder was upped to include a 1971 blue-and-white Cadillac. The next day Dottie Ross gave Lopez the title. All he had to do was take the car away from the woman (one of Smith's bail bond clients) who was currently driving it.

FBI agents provided Lopez with a Polaroid shot that appeared to show the corpse of John Calvin Baily, dead by overdose. Lopez showed the picture to Smith, along with Bailey's ID cards. Smith wasn't quite convinced. He wanted to see something in the media about Bailey's death before he would believe it.

Saturday, July 9, Cryer and Lopez met for the first of their secret rendezvous at Pease Park. Two days after the meeting, an agent from the FBI asked Cryer if he would plant a story in the *Statesman* saying that Bailey had been found murdered. "No, we can't do that," Cryer told the G-man. "But you're welcome to ask our publisher if he's OK with it." The agent talked to the publisher. The publisher's response was firm: "Absolutely not; we can't publish a story that we know isn't true."

The *Austin Citizen* was more flexible. "Charred Corpse Missing Witness?" reported that "a badly charred body in the Houston morgue may be that of confessed torch man John Calvin Bailey, a key witness in arson charges against former bail bondsman Frank Smith." "Travis County Dist. Atty. Ronald Earle confirmed today that Harris County law enforcement authorities suspect that the unrecognizably burned corpse may be Bailey's."[7]

On September 16 the FBI filed a two-page complaint specifying two counts of obstruction of justice and one count of conspiracy against Frank Smith. The complaint charged:

> That during the period of time beginning on or about June, 1977, and continuing on or about July 14, 1977, Defendant, did corruptly and by threats and force and intimidation did endeavor to influence, obstruct and impede the due administration of justice by threatening and endeavoring to kill and have killed John Calvin Bailey.

The complaint also stated that

> R. G. Lopez, a private investigator of Travis County, Texas, told affiant that the Defendant Frank Hughey Smith offered him $5,000 and a 1971 Cadillac automobile to kill John Calvin Bailey.[8]

With Smith's armed robbery trial set to begin the following Monday, the *Statesman*'s September 16, 1977, edition carried two bomb blasts on the front page: "Smith Charged in Murder Plot" and "Jailed Smith Set Up 'Hit.'" The latter was Bill Cryer's distillation of his Saturday morning meetings with R. G. Lopez.

It took some doing, but Frank was finally convinced that the hit was real, not staged. According to Lopez, Frank smiled and said, "The Lord giveth and the Lord taketh away. Blessed be the name of the Lord. I don't question the wisdom of the Lord . . ." and went on and on.

Such casual blasphemy would not have set well with Rev. Roy L. Smith, Frank's evangelical Baptist father, nor would it go down easily in the hamlet of Fredericksburg.

During the weekend hours, when R. G. Lopez's office was closed, the answering service operator received a disturbing call. "Is R. G. Lopez there?" asked the caller. "No, he's not in right now," said the receptionist. "Well, give him a message," said the caller. "Tell him to look over his shoulder. He's a dead man."[9]

The trial was heard in the Gillespie County Courthouse, an impressive granite-brick structure built in 1939 as a WPA project and quite reflective of the art deco Moderne style of public buildings during the New Deal era. One drawback, however, was that the courtroom was too big, and the acoustics worked against the ideals of truth and justice. Lawyers, jurors, reporters, and spectators often had to strain to understand the words spoken from the bench and witness stand.

Frank Smith arrives at the federal courthouse in Fredericksburg for another day of trial, dressed in what is very close to what retro stylists call a Full Cleveland.

District Judge Robert "Bob" Barton was tall and lean, a man who strode to his chambers in his cowboy boots and hung up his Stetson before donning his black robe, and he brooked no bull-shit in the courtroom. He banned cameras inside the courtroom on the first day of the trial and took other measures to tamp down the circus-like atmosphere that surrounded Frank Smith's jousting with the criminal justice system and the world at large.

Frank Smith's arrivals and departures at court were marked by clusters of reporters, jostling microphones, photographers, and television cameras. Each day the portly defendant came nattily attired 1970s style. On the first day he wore a white belt to match his white-over-black patent leather shoes. Another important style note: Ronnie Earle and his prosecutors showed up on the first day with new short haircuts. Perhaps they had heard about the 1960s in Fredericksburg, when longhaired men who had the misfortune of being caught hitchhiking west to California were taken straight to the barbershop and shorn of their flower-power manes.[10]

In their boots and Stetsons, Texas Rangers Wallace Spillar and Ronnie Brownlow appeared to be at least a head taller than the prisoner they escorted to and from court. "Ronnie had asked for them," said Twila Earle. "I asked him how he had picked the Texas Rangers who did security for Frank Smith, transporting him to the trial and walking him up and down the courthouse steps, and Ronnie said he had asked for them specifically because Frank Smith was a big man and Ronnie wanted Rangers that were taller than Frank."

Earle also coordinated the beefed-up security arrangements for the trial. Considering Smith's past record, there were genuine concerns about an escape attempt and threats to the judge, prosecutors, and witnesses. He made sure that Denise Rabb Ormand had an escort of Texas Rangers when she commuted to the trial. The courtroom and entourage were guarded by an abundance of city, county, state, and federal law officers. For most of his life Frank had treated the law as if it were a trifle, a small annoyance that could be dealt with. Ronnie Earle's show of force argued otherwise.

Monday, September 19, was devoted to jury selection. First thing Tuesday morning, the defense filed another motion for change of venue. Dunnam complained that Austin television news was available through broadcast signal and cable subscribers in Fredericksburg.[11] Ronnie Earle argued against the venue change, claiming that most people in Fredericksburg got their news from San Antonio—despite the existence of coin-operated *Statesman* stands on Fredericksburg street corners—but Barton denied Dunnam's motion without comment and ordered the testimony to begin. The jury, six men and six women, was seated at 10:35 a.m.[12]

The forty witnesses, most of whom had been subpoenaed to testify for the state, were given the oath en masse. After they were seated and some preliminary business was taken care of, Earle read the indictment, which detailed the charge in paragraphs of the usual contorted legalese, to accuse Smith of armed robbery, stating that he had, on December 3, 1976, "while in the course of committing theft and with intent to obtain and maintain control of property of Isaac A. Rabb, to wit: lawful United States currency . . . did then and there by using and exhibited a deadly weapon, to wit: a firearm, intentionally and knowingly threaten and place Isaac A. Rabb in fear of imminent bodily injury and death."[13]

Earle kept on reading the full indictment, four more long paragraphs that detailed Smith's previous felony convictions, in 1952 and 1967, in support of the habitual offender charge. And then, apparently, Earle committed an error that made a distinct impression on at least two people, both reporters covering the trial. Unfortunately, neither of them could say exactly what occurred. *Austin Citizen* reporter Ron Littlepage, who had recently written a profile of Earle, said, "I distinctly remember him getting up and starting to ask questions about [Smith's] previous convictions," which prompted a frantic reaction from the assistant prosecutors, who were "were jumping up and down trying to get him to stop."[14] "Ronnie almost blew it," said *Statesman* reporter John Sutton. "Ronnie had never tried a criminal trial and so he was reading the indictment or something, and he left something out," Sutton said. "I just remember the lawyers talking about it later on, and after that he sat down and he let somebody else handle the prosecution."

Even though Earle left the examination of witnesses and other courtroom business to Phil Nelson and assistant prosecutor

Stephen B. Edwards, there was no doubt that Earle was the coach of the team. In addition to huddling with Nelson and Edwards for strategy sessions before, during, and after long days in court, Earle was also busy keeping his most valuable witnesses on point (a challenging task) and seeing to a thousand other things that were his responsibility and couldn't be delegated to assistants.

As the trial got underway, the fate of a certain horse thief must have cast a shadow on Smith's mood. The previous week, in the same courtroom, a Killeen man named Wayne "Sonny" Yost had been tried on a charge of stealing a horse.[15] In common with Frank Smith, Sonny Yost had two previous felony convictions. One count of horse theft, a felony punishable by two to ten years, was enhanced by a habitual offender charge. In the same courtroom, with the same judge presiding, Yost was convicted on both counts and sentenced to life in prison.

Jane Rabb was the first of nine witnesses on Tuesday. Never shy about letting her emotions show, she "seemed close to tears throughout her testimony," wrote Cryer. When asked about the events that occurred after the black-over-yellow Ford LTD pulled into the parking area just after six p.m. on that fateful Friday, Jane's testimony abruptly shifted into stream-of-consciousness mode: "The next thing I know a man was in the office with a monster mask on and a jumpsuit. . . . Ike screamed, 'Oh, my God.' Everything was going around in circles. . . . My husband flew in the air and the robber was on the floor on his knees."[16]

Jane described how the masked man's trigger finger kept jerking even after he was floored by the shotgun blasts; how Ike hit him in the head with the butt of the shotgun; how people were falling over each other and wondering which one of them had been hit. Someone said there were more robbers outside, and in a flash, Ike handed his pocket pistol to Luther New and told him to cover the robber, then ran outside and shot at the two men who were shooting at him.

Ike Rabb then told his version of the events of December 3. After that, he related the incidents of arson and the harassment that preceded the robbery. The *Statesman*'s headline for the final edition on September 21, 1977, seemed to sum it up well: "Smith Swore 'Declaration of Full War.'"

Four other witnesses testified that day. Perhaps the most moving testimony was that of Jonathan, the Rabbs' fourteen-year-old son. Jonathan had driven a wrecker to lock the entrance gate that day, accompanied by Luther New's son Keith. Mc-Knight accosted the boys at the entrance gate and forced them to drive him to the office. Jonathan testified that he saw the LTD following behind the wrecker to the parking area on the right side of the chicken hut office. McKnight got out, rushed the office; Jonathan scampered under the wrecker; Keith started running, shouting, "Don't shoot, don't shoot."

"By the time the case came to trial, I think Frank being convicted was pretty much a foregone conclusion," said Bill Cryer. "For me it was kind of an amazing two weeks in this pretty, enjoyable little town. The paper sent me there with an expense account and put me up at the Sunday House, this little motel on Main Street. Ronnie's team stayed there, too. They had booked a whole section of the motel. Every morning I'd walk down to this restaurant and have breakfast. Ronnie's people would come in, with John Calvin Bailey and all these cops. Frank Smith and his lawyers would come there, too, although they didn't get out as much. The local people would look at us kind of google-eyed, like, *What the hell is this?* I think they must have thought the Mafia had come to town or something."

During strategy sessions with the assistant prosecutors and staff, Earle's assistants realized that their boss knew more about the case than they ever would. "There were characters on the fringes of this thing, and I never knew what parts, if any, they played," said Stephen Edwards. "And I never knew because none of them were on the witness list." These were the people that Ronnie Earle knew about, had grown up hearing about in Fort Worth, characters like Guy Henry Collins, who probably knew plenty about the Salvage Pool robbery, but he was not going to snitch on any of his fellow Haltom City thugs.

"You've got to remember, he doesn't have time to sit in the courtroom and listen to trials," added Edwards. "He's got every interest group in Travis County wanting something done, he's got to make public appearances, sit on committees, and so on." Strictly speaking, Earle did not have to be in Fredericksburg, but he had so much political, emotional, and philosophical capital invested in the trial, it would have been unthinkable for him not to have been. The trial put a big strain on his time. As Edwards pointed out, a great deal of Earle's job entailed going out to shake loose more appropriations from the county commissioners and the legislature to pay for the functions of a district attorney's office with such a broad mandate. That is, the Travis County DA was investigating and prosecuting not only murderers and rapists but also crimes involving state officials, corporations, and other organizations. As a result of recent legislation intended to speed up trials and appeals, two new courts had been created in Travis County, with a mandate that they be up and running by the fall. The rush to appoint new judges and fill other new positions was one of the many headaches that Earle had to juggle simultaneously while serving as field marshal for the Fredericksburg expedition.

The first few months of Earle's term were, as Twila Earle recalled, "rugged." His outsider status tended to offend and intimidate even those lawyers and staffers who had not joined the mass exodus when his surprise election victory occurred the previous spring. Before Earle gained his footing, there occurred some notable stumbles. In February, just forty-five minutes before the start of an examining trial, Earle had been forced to drop the charges against two men charged with murder in an East Austin narcotics war because the DA's office was not prepared to present evidence against the men.[17] That same week, during final arguments in a rape trial, assistant prosecutor Steve Brittain apologized to the jurors for the mistakes made by the DA's office and during the police investigation.[18] "I'd give anything to be able to show you a picture of those bruises and scratches," he said. Wishes and apologies were not enough, a juror told a *Statesman* reporter after the trial. Despite having a "gut reaction that the rape could have occurred," she said, there just was not enough hard evidence for a conviction.

There were grisly murder cases, including that of serial killer Lyle Brummett, who had murdered Dianne Roberts, a twenty-two-year-old poet and painter, the previous August, and then confessed to his involvement in the brutal killing of two teenage girls who'd gone missing in Kerrville in 1975.[19] (Brummett eventually cooperated with prosecutors and was sentenced to two life terms. As of 2021, he is still in prison.) A drifter named William Craig Riley, still at large, was indicted for the November 1976 murder of car salesman Jack Cooney III during the test drive of a Volkswagen bus, which, according to the indictment, Riley stole after he shot, "cut and disemboweled" Cooney. Earle said he felt very strongly about the case. By late May, with Riley still out there, Earle told the *Statesman* that if sufficient evidence could be produced, Riley would also be charged with kidnapping, which meant the murder charge could be increased to capital murder, which was punishable by death.[20]

By April, Earle had acquired some forward momentum in the job, launching an investigation into corruption in the State Board of Insurance and Great Commonwealth Life Insurance Corp. of Dallas. The story of this messy scandal broke on June 24, when a small army of investigators from the Texas Rangers, the DA's office, and both state and city organized crime divisions swept into the State Board of Insurance offices, without warning, and began interviewing everybody.[21]

The following Monday, Earle had an important meeting in his office with Harris County district attorney Carol Vance, to discuss a highly unusual case in which both DAs had a mutual interest. In July, after serving as a justice on the Texas Supreme Court for seven months, Donald B. Yarbrough, a Houston attorney, had been forced to resign in the face of disbarment proceedings, with over a dozen civil suits pending against him and criminal charges that included forgery of an automobile title and attempting to hire someone to murder a former business partner in Victoria.[22]

The Frank Smith trial was already underway when the county commissioners approved a budget of $15,000 ($66,632 in 2021 dollars) to pay for the prosecution.[23] The budget was based on an estimated expense of $1,000 a day to pay for food, lodging, and transportation for forty people for a trial lasting ten days, plus other unspecified costs.

The loose cannon in that group of forty people also happened to be the most indispensable witness in the case: John Calvin Bailey. Bailey was a source of amusement as well as anxiety. He was supplied enough drugs to maintain a semblance of stability, but maintaining his dope habit did nothing to control his shoplifting habit, his pranks, and the occasional shocking outburst for no apparent reason. Members of the retinue remembered how Bailey would go for midnight swims at the motel pool. As he thrashed about, his hollow leg floating nearby, he screamed about alligators being after him. Whether he was being playful or hallucinating was difficult to determine.

"He would drive the Rangers crazy with his shoplifting and stuff," remembers Twila Earle. "He would go into a convenience store with them, and he would come out and get in the car and start taking all this stuff that he had shoplifted out of his wooden

John Calvin Bailey heading up the courthouse steps in Fredericksburg to testify against Frank Smith, dressed like a character from head to toe. Bailey prided himself on his talent for writing poetry and for shoplifting.

leg. While they were in there. I remember one of them said, 'I told you I would buy that for you. Why didn't you let me?' and John Calvin said, 'I didn't want you to buy it for me.'"

Bailey was a talker. "From the minute he got up in the morning, he was talking," complained another member of Earle's team. "One morning, I remember we all rode over to get breakfast, and we were running late to get to the courthouse on time, and he was going on and on, and whoever was driving the police car, an unmarked Ford, backed up and hit a pillar on a sign, just knocked the hell out of the car, and the cop said, 'John, if you'd shut up a second I wouldn't have run into that pole.'"[24]

Nights of lost sleep over Bailey's wild antics were followed by the bombast and high drama of lead defense attorney Bill Dunnam. The infamous Wild Bill style came out on Wednesday, the third day of testimony. During his cross-examination of sheriff's deputy John Crowe, Dunnam fired off a series of blunt, accusatory questions suggesting that the prosecution of Frank Smith was part of an organized campaign or conspiracy to force Raymond Frank out of office (as if that would be a bad thing), regularly attaching the phrase "Isn't it a fact that . . ." to each question, and finally culminating with: "Isn't it a fact that if Frank Smith is convicted of this armed robbery it would go a long way toward getting Sheriff Frank out of office?" Crowe answered, "I don't know that."[25]

Perhaps Dunnam was trying to score a few points before Red Holt took the stand that afternoon. Under questioning by Nelson, Holt related the story of the robbery—how he came to be involved in it on December 2 and what had happened on the following day. He adhered to the facts he had given at Smith's bail hearing on February 2, with one notable exception: the diminutive, gruff-voiced ex-bootlegger, trader of oil and gas leases and promoter of copper Jesus and Indian chief wall decorations, testified that on the day after the robbery, Frank Smith tried to hire him to kill Ike Rabb.

Bill Cryer mentioned the murder plot in his lead for September 22: "Joseph Daniel 'Red' Holt, the star witness against former bondsman Frank H. Smith, testified Wednesday that Smith had attempted to hire him to murder the owner of the Austin Salvage Pool a day after a robbery there—allegedly masterminded by Smith—went haywire."

In an interview Cryer said the testimony was "the first public confirmation . . . that Smith wanted Ike killed in the robbery." Another important confirmation in Holt's testimony concerned Sheriff Frank's secret trip to Oklahoma City. Holt testified that when Sheriff Frank came to visit him in jail there, the sheriff placed a call to Frank Smith. Holt said that Sheriff Frank even gave him Smith's private phone number.

When Sheriff Frank was asked about the phone call, he said it was to help Holt make bail arrangements. How could that be? Smith's bonding license had been revoked by the bail bond board, of which the sheriff was a member.

"Why a grand jury didn't indict Raymond Frank after the Holt testimony is a question only Ronnie Earle could answer," said Cryer. "Maybe it's just hard to prove criminal intent. . . . But it of course doomed Raymond Frank politically. This was the almost literal smoking gun that ended his career in law enforcement and politics."

Red Holt was subjected to three hours of blistering cross-examination by Dunnam, whose obvious strategy was to somehow shift the blame to Chester Schutz as the mastermind of the robbery. The examination was like a bomb blast of stick-it notes with random ideas that failed to cohere as a narrative.[26]

Bill Cryer's journalistic instincts were stirred by the Dunnam/Smith attempt at a frame-up. After the trial adjourned for the day, he telephoned Schutz and found the four-star Austin underworld character in a responsive mood.[27] "Frank Smith has a big mouth," said Schutz, referring to Dunnam's defense strategy as well as Smith's profane attacks on Ronnie Earle. "He's just dug hisself a hole with it by calling newspapers and the TV and cussing the DA I don't know if he's all there upstairs or not."

Schutz also issued a polygraph challenge: "I'll strap on a polygraph and we'll see whether or not I had anything to do with it. I don't want to put anybody in prison—I've been there myself—but I don't believe you ought to send anybody there in your place, either."

On Friday the state called five witnesses who helped corroborate Red Holt's testimony, including a desk clerk from the E-Z Travel Motor Hotel and a motel maintenance man who had been dispatched to unclog a toilet.[28]

The Rabb family stayed in Fredericksburg for the duration of the trial. Since Jane, Ike, and Jonathan were witnesses, they were not allowed to watch the trial. Denise and Geoff watched from the gallery on some days, but with their teenage attention spans, they often found other distractions more riveting. "We went as a family, like we did everything," said Geoff. "We didn't go every day, but when we needed to be there in the courtroom, we would go. Being kids, you know, a lot of the time we would skip out on the trial and go mess around. We'd walk around, go looking for the creek, just exploring."

"During the year of the trial, I was going to school in Waco," said Denise. "So, every day that I went to Fredericksburg, the Texas Rangers came to escort me from Waco to Fredericksburg." She laughed, recalling her teenage attitude. "My perspective was, *WTF? I can drive, I know how to get there.*"

Also present in the courtroom was Dorothy Smith, always stylishly attired and poised, sitting with her daughters and son. Frank Junior was there as well. In the past year the eldest siblings, Letisha and Allan, had been putting in more hours at the wrecking yard, handling correspondence and advertising, doing the auto parts catalogues, and other jobs. Frank Junior had worked with his father since he was a snot-nosed kid, but around 1973 he'd started his own auto parts business and was no longer on good terms with Frank Senior. Dorothy had her hands full, helping Frank Senior contend with their legal problems (the current trial, civil suits, bond forfeiture appeals, and pending criminal indictments) and trying to stave off financial disaster.

Not surprisingly, the Smiths had their own interpretation of the prosecution's case. "Ronnie Earle wanted to make a legend for himself," said Letisha Taylor. "He knew my dad had connections with the big Mafia and that's what he wanted. . . . The feds came to my dad and said, *If you'll say this and this and this . . . all this can go away and you can go home.* My dad knew that could never work out. It would've been a virtual death sentence for my family. We wouldn't have lasted any time at all."

Frank and Dorothy Smith had often suggested through the media that Earle was motivated by his ambitions to seek a higher political office and that prosecuting a major celebrity like Smith would bring him the fame and recognition he needed. In reality, Frank Smith's criminal actions were an insult to Earle's moral sensibility and his ideals of justice. By prosecuting Smith in district court, shutting down the predatory bail bondsmen in Travis County, and investigating numerous other criminal acts that could result in additional indictments, Earle was merely acting within his responsibilities as the district attorney in Travis County. Smith's ties to organized crime were already being investigated by federal and other law enforcement agencies. Earle would assist those efforts when appropriate.

Monday morning, the second week of the Frank Smith trial, began with more damning corroboration of Red Holt's testimony. Two Austin attorneys testified that they had seen and spoken to Frank Smith and Red Holt together at Piccadilly Cafeteria the morning after the robbery.[29] Next, a sharp-dressed, whisker-trimmed John Calvin Bailey took the stand to bring it all home for the state. Bailey told the jury about the hiring, planning, and botched execution of the October 18 arson at the Austin Salvage Pool, for which Smith had hired Bailey and two other men.

During his seven hours of testimony that day, Bailey said Smith had complained to him about the botched robbery, asserting that "a nine-year-old . . . from Arkansas with a steak knife" could've done a better job than the "people from Fort Worth." Smith also asked him to make a second attempt to burn down the Austin Salvage Pool. According to Bailey, these memorable exchanges occurred in Smith's office on Christmas Eve, the same day that Bill Cryer was hanging around the office collecting quotes and impressions for his coming story, "A Man with Power," published in the *Statesman* the day after Christmas. Bailey was certain about the Christmas Eve date, he said, because earlier in the holiday season, he'd been locked up on a charge of aggravated robbery, but on December 24, Smith signed his bail.

Under cross-examination by Dunnam, Bailey again stated that he sometimes sold drugs to support himself and that he frequented a certain downtown bar (JJJ's Tavern on Sixth Street) where he peddled stolen cigarettes and original poems for a dollar apiece.[30] Dunnam tried to get Bailey to connect Chester Schutz with the robbery, but Bailey answered that he and Schutz had only met a few times and were not close friends. Dunnam also pointed out that Bailey had seven felony convictions on his record and four felonies had been dismissed by the state in exchange for his testimony. Dunnam asked Bailey if he would rather have $10,000 or be imprisoned for life as a habitual criminal. Bailey replied: "I'd take the $10,000 and hire an attorney like you to defend me." The exchange triggered smiles among jurors and spectators alike.

Dunnam wanted to use Cryer to rebut part of Bailey's testimony. As Cryer wrote on Tuesday ("Writer Testifies in Smith Trial"), Dunnam asked if he was at Smith's office the same time Bailey was there on Christmas Eve. Cryer answered that he had been with Smith nearly all day, working on a story. Asked what the three of them had talked about, Cryer said, "My recollection of the conversation is that it concerned Mr. Bailey's wooden leg, a letter to the editor he had written and some poetry."[31]

Cryer could neither confirm nor deny that a private conversation between Smith and Bailey had occurred. In an interview, he pointed out that the bail bond office contained both a waiting room and Smith's private office, and such a conversation could have occurred without his knowledge.

The mood in the Frank Smith camp must have been a little uplifted by Cryer's testimony, but Ronnie Earle had saved a surprise witness who was sure to bring them back down to earth. Charles Garner, an old friend of Frank's from the car business, had been one of his coconspirators in the federal car-theft case in 1967.[32]

Garner told an interesting story. Sometime in the fall of 1976, before Frank hired Bailey to torch the Salvage Pool, Smith had outlined a more elaborate arson scheme with Garner. Smith had taken him to the Austin Salvage Pool, he said, and "he just told me what he wanted done and asked if I knew any people he could trust." Garner described what was to be a three-man job, one to drive a truck loaded with drums of a kerosene/gasoline mixture and two others to use a pump to spray the fluid on the mobile trailer and late-model cars, setting the fires as the arsonists stealthily exited the yard.

Garner testified that he had recommended George Harding (then married to Smith's bond office manager, Dottie Ross) for the gig, saying, "Old George is always wanting to do something for money." Garner had not been able to go through with the job, however, because he was arrested, along with four other Austin men, for conspiring to deal illegally in firearms, which they had stored in wrecked cars in their possession.[33]

Harding and four others were sentenced May 12, 1977, but the charges against Garner were dropped in exchange for his testimony against Frank Smith. At his turn for cross-examination on Tuesday, Dunnam jumped on this point, accusing Garner of making up his story in exchange for a Get-Out-of-Jail-Free card. Garner was having none of it.

"I felt that I had all the hell that I needed and didn't need to share Mr. Frank Smith's or anyone else's," Garner said.

Dunnam tried again. He asked Garner, who was forty-six, how old his wife was.

"Thirty-three," he said. "She's pretty."

Did that mean Garner would say anything to avoid going to prison?

"Never in my life have I ever wanted to go to the penitentiary," Garner replied. "But I don't intend to stand up here and perjure myself."

The witness was excused.

Next, Nelson recalled Ike Rabb and went over some additional questions about the robbery. At last he asked Ike to identify items of physical evidence relating to the robbery. Each item was placed on a table in front of the jury before it was named and explained: the coveralls the robbers had worn; the masks, including the monkey mask worn by Willie McKnight; and two large pistols. By the time the last item was presented, the clock showed 3:04 p.m. The state rested its case.

The defense team did not have to convince the jury that Frank Smith was a morally upstanding citizen, nor did they have to explain every one of the client's strange actions; no, the only imperative was to knock a leg or two out from under the prosecutor's table. Attacking the credibility of the state's star witnesses, Bailey and Holt, was not terribly difficult. Dunnam's Fredericksburg co-counsels would contribute to that effort.

The defense's effort to paint Isaac Rabb as the source of ill will in the case began with the first witnesses Dunnam called. Two of them had been employed as legal assistants to Smith's attorney, Broadus Spivey, in the fall of 1976, when Spivey was preparing to file Smith's civil suit against Rabb. The first to testify, Jim Moore, was a UT graduate and former UT football player.[34] Moore testified that on a visit to the Austin Salvage Pool in late October, after the arson fire, he observed that Rabb was unfriendly and hostile to Frank Smith.

Dunnam asked Moore what he observed when Smith asked Rabb why he refused to do business with him: "Rabb told Frank,

'It's none of your business. I just don't want your business,'"
Moore stated. "Frank was very courteous the whole time. In fact,
I was scared. Mr. Rabb was very rude."[35]

Dunnam called Pat Kelly, also a former UT football player.
Kelly, who had accompanied Moore and Smith to Rabb's wrecking yard on that day, also stated that Rabb seemed to be the ag-
gressor in the Smith/Rabb relationship.

During cross-examination, however, each young man was
asked if he thought he might have interpreted the situation a
bit differently had he known that Smith "had something to do
with that burned out trailer you saw out there."

"Yes," replied Moore. "Most certainly so." Kelly gave a similar
answer.

Wallace Crowder, a wrecker driver and nineteen-year veteran
of the Houston Police Department, was called as the defense ex-
pert on John Calvin Bailey, whom he had known during his time
in the burglary division and regarded as an inveterate criminal
and dope addict. "Do you know John Calvin Bailey's reputation
for truth and veracity?" asked Dunnam. "Yes, sir," replied the
witness. "It is very poor. Very poor."

A veteran auto salvage dealer, Crowder could have made a
very credible witness for the defense. But his responses during
a brief cross-examination by Phil Nelson could not have left a
good impression with the jury.

> NELSON: How long have you known Frank Smith?
> CROWDER: I don't know Frank Smith—who is Frank
> Smith—I don't know Frank Smith.
> NELSON: You don't know Frank Smith at all?
> CROWDER: Yeah, I know a bunch of Smiths, but I can't
> think of a Frank Smith.
> NELSON: You never heard of Frank Smith in Austin,
> the defendant in this case?
> CROWDER: From where?

NELSON: From Austin—the defendant in this case.
CROWDER: No...
NELSON: You are in the wrecker business, and you
         don't know Frank Smith?
CROWDER: No. (*TvFS*, 1445–1455)

Dr. Charles Burke, a Fredericksburg physician, was called as the local authority on drug addiction. After a brief back-and-forth on the history and effects of heroin and other opium derivatives, Burke and Dunnam zeroed in on the unique horrors of cold-turkey heroin withdrawal.

Burke stated that no one ever stopped taking heroin unless forced to do so. The implication was that John Calvin Bailey had been threatened with cold turkey or even subjected to it for the purpose of obtaining his cooperation. The exchange quickly veered into caricature.

Dunnam asked what an addict might do if suddenly cut off from drugs.

"There is no limit to what he would do," answered Burke.

"Would you say that a little louder?" asked Dunnam.

"There is no limit to what he would do: lie, cheat, steal, kill; if he needed it, he would do it" (*TvFS*, 1470–1483).

The defense also made a concerted effort to prove an alternative version of Frank Smith's movements in the period of time before and after the robbery. John Pfluger, much-loved banker to the Smith family, testified that Smith came to the bank alone on the morning of December 3, contradicting Red Holt's testimony that they were together.

Smith claimed he returned to the bank to cash a check for over $20,000 and left at about 3:30 p.m. This was corroborated by two other bank employees (*TvFS*, 1455–1469).

Another layer of complexity regarding Smith's alleged movements on December 3 was provided by witness Andrew Jacob Rogers, a former state legislator from Childress (a Panhandle town of six thousand that in the mid-2010s was ranked as the ninth most conservative city in the United States), and Ed Raspberry, a pipe fitter and salesman from Burkett whom Smith described as a "John Bircher."[36] Rogers testified that his car was being repaired at Smith's wrecking yard on December 3. Smith had offered him a ride to his bonding office and the use of his phone. The trip downtown involved several detours, Rogers said—Smith had errands to run, including a brief visit to his aunt's house, additional stops along the way, and more trips later in the day. Rogers testified that he and Smith were together again at about 3:15 p.m.

Witness Raspberry claimed he was with Smith between 10:00 and 11:30 a.m. that day and again between 3:00–3:15 p.m.

Austin in the 1970s was still small enough that a person could drive around town without encountering gridlock around every corner. You could cruise from one end of town to the other doing errands of various kinds in one average, casual, sun-kissed morning. Was it possible to do all the things, go all the places, that Frank Smith claimed he had done on the day of the robbery? The jury would have to decide.

Sam Houston Johnson took the stand midafternoon. Under direct examination by Dunnam, Johnson was asked about a phone conversation he had with Frank Smith on Christmas Eve. Johnson said that Smith had called to invite him to Christmas dinner. In the same conversation, he said, Frank mentioned that Bailey was in his office. Smith complained that Bailey owed him money, so he was going to go off his bond and make Bailey spend Christmas in jail. Johnson said, "Oh, don't put him back in jail. Let him spend Christmas day out."

Dunnam asked Johnson about a story that Bailey had stolen some prescription pills from him at the Alamo Hotel. Johnson didn't seem bothered by the theft and expressed uncertainty about the story's veracity. The first time the theft was reported to him, Johnson's response was, "Oh, well." He would just get the prescription refilled again.

The old pol, wracked by lung cancer and various infirmities, scarred by political knife fights and the tragic arc of the Johnson family legacy, seemed fond of the court jester antics of the skinny poet who cleaned his offices to pay for his board at the hotel. "John Calvin . . . he wrote poetry," Johnson said, "and he carried on a lot of stuff, you know, and he used my phone—I have a private line—and he called up different ones and read them his poetry. . . . He didn't do anything harmful. . . . I will say I didn't mind hearing some of the poems because it was kind of next to comedy."

Ironically, Johnson offered no words of support for the man on trial. When Nelson asked if he and Frank Smith were "social friends," Johnson answered no, he was not. "I have just known him," he said (*TvFS*, 1554–1565).

It was late afternoon when the defendant took the stand. He wore a pale green leisure suit and dark green shirt with the collar open wide. Since the first day of the trial, he had been sitting quietly, following the testimony, dipping snuff.[37] Sometimes he would throw a grin to his wife and family members. He would glance at Bill Cryer and occasionally favor him with a wink.

During recesses, as people moved about in the corridor, friends and family of the opposing sides inevitably brushed against each other. Only rarely did a flare-up occur, the offended parties bristling like the prickly pear cactus that whiskered the stony, rolling landscape of the old German settlement.

Smith's decision to testify ran against prevailing wisdom in such cases, and it even surprised some people who knew the man and knew he should have known better. Frank was the famously affable guy, the ultimate glad-handing, impossible-to-dislike, self-effacing, funny-bone-tickling giant. Smith may have thought, *If anyone can sway the jurors, I can pull off the old magic.* Dunnam was too smart to think it was a good idea, but at this point in the trial he may have thought, *What does it matter? Let Frank try to have the last word.*

Under direct examination by Dunnam, Smith rambled for five minutes or more about his hardscrabble beginnings, his family, his children, how his mother and his father, "a pastor of a Baptist church in Waco," took custody of a son by his first marriage until his mother died of a hospital error, and afterward, Frank and his mother's sister, Aunt Sally Mae Hughey, moved out to her farm to raise the son, Frank Hughey Smith Jr.[38]

Ladling on the country-lawyer charm, Dunnam inquired about the sharing of responsibilities for "the little fellow" and where "that boy" resided at present. That "little fellow" was now thirty-one years old, an heir to his father's tree-trunk physique who had served in the army and served time in prison for selling LSD. "That boy," who never got along too well with the father who went to the pen when he was six years old, was seated in the courtroom with the rest of the Smith family.

Frank Senior was on the stand for two hours that day. The way he told it, he was the victim in the business feud with Ike Rabb. He alleged that Rabb was an unethical, combative crank who was trying to run him out of business. Worst of all, he, Frank Smith, had been set up for robbery or murder during the bloody fiasco at the Austin Salvage Pool.

Frank did admit that he had given Red Holt a check for $500 in 1976. The check was for hunting bail jumpers, he said. During that visit, Holt had tried to interest him in some oil and gas leases. "I don't mean to be offensive," he told the jury, "but I told him the only oil I had was what was on my head, and the only gas I had was what was on my stomach, and I didn't know anything about the oil and gas business." The legendary Depression-era folksinger Huddie Ledbetter, better known as Lead Belly, had won his release from prison by serenading the governor. Perhaps Frank Smith thought he could win another pardon by telling bad jokes.

On Friday, December 2, 1976, Smith was surprised, he said, to find Red Holt waiting in his office, drinking his whiskey, and reading a stack of newspaper clippings about his problems with the Austin Salvage Pool. They went to dinner at the Hoffbrau Steakhouse, a hip-pocket-sized grill on West Sixth that had made few concessions to the decades that passed since it first opened in 1932. Red took the whisky bottle along and continued to imbibe from it as they dined. Frank mentioned to him that he had to take a large amount of money to the Rabbs the next day, "probably twenty thousand dollars or twenty-five thousand."

Friday morning, Red popped up at the wrecking yard, Smith said, and later Chester Schutz came by. Frank said he would meet them at La Tapatia, the Mexican restaurant on East Sixth, and pick up the tab. Chester said he would bring "the Black Widow," meaning Robyn Schnautz.

Dunnam guided his client through the day's schedule, including the distances between various points on the alibi map. Frank answered questions about how things went at the Salvage Pool during the time he was there, paying for the cars.

"I mean, it was a very unfriendly attitude out there," Smith said. "I was anxious to get away from out of there." As he was leaving, he saw no other cars on the road, he said.

Downtown again, Frank ran more errands, he said, before arriving back at the bond office, where once again he found Red Holt making himself at home, drinking his whiskey. He had no idea that Holt had been involved in a robbery, he stated. The next day Frank took Red and another friend, Doc Parten, now deceased, to Three Sisters, a cozy Chinese cafe on Burnet Road near the State School for the Blind. Smith gave Red a check for $300. It was for help finding some bond skips, he said, not expenses incurred on a trip to Austin to participate in an armed robbery.

Thursday morning, Dunnam completed his direct examination of Smith with questions about Christmas Eve, when Cryer and Bailey were in his office. Did he have a private conversation— about arson, perhaps—outside the presence of Cryer? Smith answered, "The only place that I went at all [where] he wasn't that I can think of, and have racked my brain, I might have gone to the bathroom a couple of times when he didn't go." "And did Bailey go with you to the bathroom?" Smith said no. Dunnam said, "That's all," and passed the witness.

Phil Nelson had handled the lion's share of the examinations so far, employing his instincts and intuition like a chess master. Reporter Carol Fowler was a great admirer of Nelson's talent. "Phil Nelson was the absolute master of minutiae," she said. "He could run the Lord's Prayer on the head of a pin." Fowler might have also added that Nelson had the compositional talents of a dramatist, because from the first question he asked Frank Smith, tension began to build.

> NELSON: Mr. Smith, you want to be completely
> honest with these jurors, don't you?
> SMITH: I certainly do.
> NELSON: You have said that several times voluntarily
> as you testified, haven't you?
> SMITH: I have tried to be as honest with them as
> I am capable of being, as my memory
> will let me.

Nelson continued this tact, asking, "Are you concealing something from them? Are you hiding anything from this jury?" Smith: "I'm not hiding anything." Nelson kept on, like a priest urging his confessor to come clean. Finally, Nelson brought up the names of the state's star witnesses, John Calvin Bailey, Red Holt, and Charles Garner. Nelson reminded Smith that he and Dunnam had gone out of their way to "attack and impeach" the reputations of Bailey, Holt, and Garner because they had been convicted of felony crimes. Smith had belittled Bailey for being "a dope addict." Red Holt was a "sneak thief . . . a con man . . . a burglar of little old ladies in apartments."

Dunnam objected to the questions and was overruled. Dunnam called for a mistrial—denied. He did this repeatedly, interrupting the testimony.

If Smith wanted to be "absolutely truthful," Nelson said, "then why haven't you told them where you met Red Holt?" "I haven't been asked that question yet," said Smith. Nelson asked the question. "I met Red Holt in the United States Federal Penitentiary in Leavenworth, Kansas, in approximately the latter part of 1969," said Smith. "That's been in the paper 10,000 times."

Nelson asked Smith, "Would you turn around and tell them the truth, the whole truth, and nothing but the truth—just look at them and tell them under oath?"

"I'm already under oath," Smith complained. Then he turned to face the jury box and said, "I'm going to tell the truth, the whole truth, and nothing but the truth, as best that my memory will allow me."

Nelson then read the charge from the 1967 conviction, starting with, "Are you one and the same Frank Smith . . ." and ending with, "are you one and the same person?"

SMITH: I am the same person.

NELSON: Were you sentenced to a term of five years on each count?

SMITH: Yes, I was.

NELSON: Did you meet Red Holt in Leavenworth Federal Correctional Institute in Kansas?

SMITH: I did meet Red Holt in the federal penitentiary in Kansas.

NELSON: Was Chester Schutz there, too?

SMITH: He was there some of the time I was there.

Around this point in the transcript, you can feel the energy start to drain from Frank Smith, feel his mojo fading. Nelson, in total control, picked up the pace. He tangled with Smith over the concept of salvage titles and whether or not they were true titles, Nelson showing off considerable expertise on the subject, while Smith evoked a sort of fetish about terms. Nelson steered the discussion back to the point at which Smith had threatened

Ike Rabb with "war—all-out war." Smith admitted having said those words, but by war, he said, he only meant, "I went down to an attorney, paid him money to file a civil litigation."

About an hour later in the transcript, one can sense Smith winding down, while Nelson's questions bristle with energy, perhaps even a bit of giddiness. The first assistant district attorney showed Smith State's Exhibit No. 99, a check from Frank Smith to John Calvin Bailey in the amount of $600 and dated October 18, 1976.

NELSON: And did you give him that check?

SMITH: I did.

NELSON: And that just happened to be the date that the arson occurred?

SMITH: I am not aware of what date the arson occurred, other than what I read in the paper and heard testified here to, but I did give him that check for $600.

NELSON: And did you write on that check that it was an advance to chase bond jumpers—what did you write on there, by way of a note?

SMITH: "Investigations, bond jumpers."

NELSON: Now, is that John Bailey the same John Bailey that you hold in such disdain?

SMITH: It is.

NELSON: The dope addict?

SMITH: It is.

NELSON: And the thief?

SMITH: It is.

NELSON: And you gave him a check for $600 to go chase bond jumpers for you?

SMITH: I did.

Dunnam objected, citing a number of reasons, and without waiting for Barton to rule on the objection, called for a mistrial. Both were denied. Testimony resumed:

NELSON: Haven't you told this jury the first thing
John Calvin Bailey does when he gets
money is go off and buy dope?

SMITH: That's true; he does.

NELSON: Yet you expect this jury to believe you are
going to give him $600 to go chase bond
jumpers for you?

Bill Cryer, who was able to pack a tremendous amount of information into every daily dispatch for the *Statesman* (sometimes more than one article per day), aptly described the end of the proceedings on Friday:

> Testimony in the trial ended at 5:07 p.m. yesterday after a lineup of Texas Rangers, Texas Department of Public Safety agents, police officers, and a former district attorney trooped into the courtroom to say that Smith's reputation for "truth and veracity" was bad.

> Smith, who clashed with First Assistant District Attorney Phil Nelson for about six hours during cross-examination, appeared calm as he left the courtroom, stopping to hug his elderly aunt, kiss his 17-year-old daughter, and wink at reporters.[39]

That Friday, the tenth and final day of the trial, was the longest, stretching a half hour past midnight for a dramatic, nerve-quivering finale. Final arguments concluded at 2:40 p.m., the jury deliberated for three and a half hours, and it returned just after 6:20 p.m. with a verdict of guilty. Bill Cryer rushed from the courtroom to phone in his story. His writing vividly captured the emotional responses that whipsawed through the room.

> Moments after the guilty verdict was read by the district clerk at 6:20 p.m., Smith's daughters, 17 and 8, began sobbing uncontrollably.

They were led outside the courtroom, where their mother was waiting.

Mrs. Smith did not return to the courtroom when the verdict came in. Instead she heard the jurors' decision from a reporter as he dashed to phone in his story.

District Judge Robert Barton had to ask the bailiff to take the jury out of the room until order could be restored. As the jurors filed out, grim-faced, the loud sobbing of the young girls echoed through the cavernous courtroom.[40]

Steve Edwards, second assistant district attorney, was an unsung MVP of the prosecution team. Rarely heard from during the trial, Edwards was an experienced and aggressive prosecutor. Earlier in the day, he showed off his flair for the dramatic when he delivered the state's first final argument. Conceding that defense witnesses Holt, Bailey, and Garner had criminal records, Edwards referred to them as "dime a dozen" crooks and said, "Do we try to get rid of the thugs one by one until none are left or do we try to get rid of the one that is hiring them?"[41]

The Smiths were sitting in the front row when Edwards pointed at them and said, "Whatever grief his family is feeling was caused by the actions of Frank Smith." Dorothy Smith got up and stomped out of the room. After the verdict, the jury was dismissed again as the attorneys argued technical points of the habitual offender charge in a session that lasted several hours. The issues were settled by around 11:30 p.m., and the jurors were sent off for a final time to deliberate on that charge, which counted both the 1967 federal conspiracy conviction and Smith's 1952 armed robbery conviction in Falls County. At 12:30 a.m. the jury returned with a verdict of guilty and an automatic sentence of life in prison.

Earlier that evening, after the first verdict was announced, Jane Rabb was so overcome with tears and tremors that Ike had to help her leave the courtroom. Out in the hallway, Dorothy

Smith felt no sympathy: "Why would Mrs. Rabb cry? She won her victory." After the second verdict was read, Jane was still fighting to remain composed. Turning to Cryer, her voice faltering, she said, "You know, there is no victory."[42]

In the midst of all the drama, one individual appeared calm and unaffected: Frank Smith. "I was able to go up and talk to him," said Cryer. "He was kind of fatalistic through the whole thing, but he never lost his sense of humor. It was dark sometimes, of course. But he was kind of modest and self-deprecating. He was likeable. He was a strange, strange man."

Later, during a break in a hearing for a new trial, Smith came over to the prosecutors table to visit with Steve Edwards. "We talked just like two people," said Edwards. "It sounds kind of strange, but everybody liked Frank. Everybody liked Frank, they just thought he was crooked as hell."

Ronnie Earle, the inexperienced district attorney, had won his first case, one of the biggest criminal cases in the history of Travis County. Granted, it had been a team effort, the fruit of a productive relationship between Earle, Phil Nelson, Steve Edwards, and many other supporting players, but from the beginning, the case was seen as Ronnie Earle's to lose.

On the first day of the trial, Bill Cryer had written short blurbs for each of the principal figures involved. Ronnie Earle, he wrote, "is the 35-year-old wunderkind liberal politician with little actual courtroom experience who will cut his prosecutorial eye teeth on possibly the biggest case he will ever have to try. He will be watched by the courthouse pros, some of whom are waiting gleefully for him to fall on his face."[43] Time would render the middle portion of that description ironic (predicting the prosecution of Frank Smith as Earle's "biggest case"). Earle was reelected every four years for three decades, during which time he would become a national figure, prosecuting not only major criminal cases but corrupt politicians and powerful CEOs.

"The whole time during the trial and leading up to the trial, I was meeting with Phil Nelson, the first assistant district attorney," said Steve Edwards in an interview for this book. "We were working on facts, evidence, and witnesses, but Ronnie was focusing on a lot of things that had nothing to do with evidence or trial. He liked to figure out the big picture. Like, *Could this be connected to that? Or this other thing connected to that?*"

"Ronnie running a meeting was a thing to behold," said Twila Earle. "Ronnie thoroughly enjoyed people, problem solving, and laughing, and his meetings were highly productive." Early in the meeting he would name the elephant in the room, breaking the tension with a joke about it. "People usually left in good spirits and with a sense of purpose, confidence, and cooperation. Things got done."

The courthouse cynics, who harped on the fact that Earle had never tried a case in court before, ended up being dazzled by Earle's people skills, perhaps realizing that he had come by those skills honestly, through life experience, empathy, and thousands of interactions with the people from all walks of life who had come before him as a judge in municipal court.

Twila Earle also shared one of the lesser-known, character-revealing stories about the Fredericksburg experience. After the start of the trial, Bailey started having cold feet about testifying. "He got concerned for his safety," Twila said. Unpredictable on his best days, Bailey became ever more erratic as his fear of being murdered by one of Smith's henchmen increased. Fortunately, Ronnie Earle found an unconventional though instinctive solution.

"Bailey wrote poetry," Twila said, "and Ronnie also wrote poetry. So, Ronnie and John Calvin would get together and read their poems to each other." The effort helped cement Bailey's trust of Earle and fix his intention to adhere to his end of the bargain, testifying against Frank Smith under threat of death. It must have been a first—the prosecutor who wrote the judicial article for the state constitution convention of 1974, in a poetry-sharing relationship with a one-legged junkie shoplifter. Just goes to show, Earle was a man of many dimensions.

AFTERMATH

On October 12, 1977, the *Fredericksburg Standard* printed a letter of appreciation for the "courtesy, patience and hospitality"
extended to the Travis County District Attorney's office and
the large contingent of law enforcement representatives "who
more or less established a temporary home in Gillespie County"
during the trial of Frank Smith. "The sole regret I've heard is
that the majority of us involved in the trial got to see only the
east and west ends of Highway 290, and not the rest of your
beautiful city. . . . We plan to return someday soon—as individual visitors—to see more of your fine city, renew friendships
made during our stay, and sample again your outstanding hospitality." The letter was signed, "Very truly yours, Ronald Earle,
District Attorney, Travis County."

In November Frank Smith was back in court in Fredericksburg for three marathon sessions as his attorneys argued for a
new trial.[1] Nelson and Edwards argued against the motion; Judge
Barton denied it. After Thanksgiving dinner in Fritztown on
November 29, Frank was whisked off to Huntsville, four days shy
of the anniversary of the robbery fiasco, to begin his life sentence.

The millions that came Smith's way during the peak of his bail
bond business were mostly gone, although some assets had been

squirrelled away by various means, with the assistance of friendly bankers, lawyers, and other Smith family partisans. Meanwhile, Sheriff Raymond Frank, who had been instrumental in Smith making his millions, was left in a mess of his own making. Although no indictments had come from either the federal or county grand juries, Frank's reputation was permanently ruined. In one of the more malodorous messes he had created, the sheriff had hired, on Frank's command, Everett Walter DeLong as a medic in the jail dispensary. The hiring was astonishingly bad form, as DeLong was on probation for selling dangerous drugs in California. His criminal record in that state also included hiring men to beat up a woman, fraud, burglary, perjury, criminal conspiracy, and illegal wiretapping. In an insurance case in 1967, DeLong had been found not guilty by reason of insanity and confined two years in a state hospital for the criminally insane. Among the inmates at the jail, however, DeLong was popular due to his carefree distribution of happy pills.[2]

The story of DeLong's hiring by the sheriff would begin to make more sense after it was revealed that DeLong had met Frank Smith when he was working at an auto parts store in Waco. Smith told Sheriff Frank to give DeLong a job, so he did, and DeLong bragged about it: *Frank Smith got me this job.*

Sheriff Frank not only refused to terminate DeLong but sought a raise for him, thus bringing more attention to the scandal. When a whistleblower reported additional inconvenient facts about DeLong, Sheriff Frank fired the whistleblower. When the county commissioners complained that the job description for the jail's dispensary medic required that the applicant be a *qualified registered nurse* and DeLong was neither, the sheriff changed the job description.

Not surprisingly, when Frank ran for reelection in 1980, he lost. By a lot. The veteran APD detective and Baptist youth minister Doyne Bailey campaigned on a message of professionalism and the principles of basic law enforcement and won by a wide margin. Voters went for Bailey again in 1984 and 1988. In July 1992 Bailey was poised for another sure victory when he answered the call of Governor Ann Richards to serve as director of the state criminal justice division.

Reporter Bill Cryer got a salary bump after the Frank Smith trial. He was proud of that $20 a week raise and didn't mind being praised by the city editor, Ray Mariotti, in an op-ed that appeared on October 30. Mariotti wrote that Ike Rabb had recently visited him at the *Statesman* to express his great appreciation for the reporters who worked so hard to unearth the truth—particularly Bill Cryer. Ike asked if there was anything he could do to help him. "We'll give Rabb credit for Cryer's next raise in a couple of weeks," wrote Mariotti. "But otherwise, Bill and the newspaper were satisfied that they were doing a job. Bill wasn't playing policeman. He was keeping his readers informed."[3]

Cryer's work at the *Statesman* shows that he was a gifted wordsmith in addition to being a thorough and dedicated journalist, but like many professional writers, he is modest and unassuming about his work. In conversation he is more likely to tell stories about the big mistakes he has made during his career rather than boast of his achievements and awards.

"I readily admit to being largely incompetent in all of my jobs," he said in an interview. "But I do have a knack for being tall male with regular features . . . and a habit of promptly answering telephone calls." Serendipity, he said, "is the great resume-builder."

In December 1982 Bill ran into Ann Richards at the Armadillo Christmas Bazaar. At the time she was the newly elected state treasurer, and the campaign to win that office had been reported on by Cryer. "She was beaming in her new glory that day, and we enthusiastically exchanged tales about the campaign," he said. The next morning, the phone rang. It was Ann. She needed a press guy. Was he available?

"Whatever you're doing, it's not going to be as much fun as working for me," she told him. He took the job and continued through her four years as governor of Texas. "She was right," he said. "It was the most fun of any job I ever had."

In December 1977 Ike and Jane hired attorney Lee Yeakel to file a $1.5 million suit for damages against Frank Smith.[4] Unfortunately, neither John Calvin Bailey nor Red Holt was available to testify in person, so Yeakel submitted a transcript of the armed robbery trial in their place, but the judge was not impressed. The Rabbs settled out of court for a paltry $3,000.

The Rabb family is made of stern stuff. They persevered with their lives and their work during the "This Is War" years with their sanity and souls intact and reaped the rewards of a successful, exponentially growing business. The efficiency and professionalism of their brokerage operation impressed both local vendors and insurance company associates, and soon the salvage pool business model became the standard in the auto recycling industry.

Locally, the volume of business for Austin Salvage Pool steadily increased along with the rapid rate of growth in the Austin area, fueled by the city's reputation as a mecca for musicians and other creative artists, which in turn, accelerated the growth of Austin's high-tech industry, compounded as word spread of the beauty of the Hill Country and Austinites' passionate respect for the environment. Within a decade or so, Austin gained a reputation as one of the coolest places on the planet.

Most of the new residents and visitors to Austin drove automobiles—machines on which collisions and natural disasters take a regular toll. "In the beginning, we'd have fifteen to two dozen cars that we would auction every two weeks," Ike said, compared to the current-day total of around eight hundred autos sold every week.

"We looked forward to natural disasters," Denise said, explaining that "there was a windfall whenever there was a flood, or a hail storm. We'd have high-volume total losses." In 2015, Geoff said, they processed three thousand cars from Houston that were totaled in Hurricane Harvey.

In 2001, after over thirty years in business, Austin Salvage Pool was bought by Insurance Auto Auctions, Inc., an international corporation.[5] Announcing the sale, IAA issued a statement saying that the owners of Austin Salvage Pool "have run an excellent facility and have wonderful people." Three of those wonderful people, siblings Denise, Geoff, and Reneé, remained with IAA after the transfer. As of 2020, Ike Rabb still owned and leased most of the Dalton property to the corporation. As for the other portion of the tract, Geoff chuckled and offered that he and Ike have their "special archives" parked there.

Sadly, Jonathan perished in a car crash in 1982, only nineteen years old. The passing of Jane Rabb in 2011 also hit the family hard. Death unexpectedly claimed the eldest sibling, Anne Marie Wagnor-White, in the spring of 2020.

Denise confided that they were "fighting off a wave of shocking sadness," a response that seemed of a piece with her descriptions of the emotional reckonings of the family over the years.

"A multitude of really awful, unfathomable things happened to this little family," said Denise. In the past, she said, she had only looked at the Frank Smith episodes as "a scary part of our lives." Her own hope, she said, was for a book that would "be something for my kids and grandkids to know how crazy things were, and how brave Mom and Dad were, fighting hard to stop a crazy man and stay alive."

The family's ordeals with Frank Smith were "kind of surreal, for sure," said Geoff Rabb, "but I tend to just look at things at face value and just deal with them and remain kind of realistic about it and not get too emotional. I mean, yeah, it was upsetting but our family always had a strong bond, and we're there for each other at all times."

Dorothy Smith filed for divorce after the trial—a fairly transparent attempt at a shell game to protect the Smiths' assets from seizure by any of several governmental bodies. For example, Smith owed the county $121,000 in bond forfeitures.[6] Through various means, including a family trust and transfer of ownership, Frank and Dorothy had been maneuvering to protect their assets since the beginning of 1977. Frank told Bill Cryer that in early 1978, his interest in his wrecking yard was sold to an "Arab interest." Cryer found that the property had been sold to a firm called Abu Dhabi, Inc.; the main principals were "Smith's aunt, a woman in Canada and a man with a post office box in Abu Dhabi." The IRS snatched up the home on Hunters Lane. The ornate, hand-carved Mexican desk and furnishings in the bail bond office were seized and sold at auction for nickels on the dollar. Frank's desk brought a paltry $50.

The *Statesman* reported in January 1978 that Dorothy had dropped the divorce petition. A related story in the adjacent column reported that the gun smuggling charges against Frank Smith's former friend and conspirator, Charles Garner, had just been dismissed.[7]

Less than two months after Frank Smith was found guilty of armed robbery in the Salvage Pool case, Allan Beto Smith, his fifteen-year-old son, was arrested for robbing a convenience store, armed with a knife.[8] Named after the Texas governor who had pardoned his father and the prison director who'd befriended him, Allan continued to have unconstructive encounters with the law. He did some prison time and died in 2018 at the age of fifty-six.

Through the late 1970s and early 1980s, Frank Smith's presence was periodically required in Travis County court proceedings, necessitating an overnight stay at the jail where the keepers who knew him so well regularly tallied long lists of "refused to comply" violations. The occasion for one of those trips was the need for him to testify at a hearing for a notorious meth addict, who was eventually executed by lethal injection for killing an Austin police officer in a hail of AK-47 fire on a normally sedate and cozy street in Travis Heights.[9] Another was a hearing with the IRS, and another regarded an abusive prison warden who was later fired.[10] According to Smith he was acting as an undercover prison reformer. Such comings and goings were all reported in the *Statesman* but were relegated to the Metro section of the paper, the B section. Frank Smith had just one more front page left in his lifetime.

Saturday night, June 3, 1978, Tressa Granger and Letisha Taylor had a fun time on the Drag (a section of Guadalupe Street that borders the UT campus), just being teenagers, doing teenage girl stuff. At the end of the night they parted and went to their respective homes. Letisha arrived at 11402 Hunters Lane just before midnight to find sheriff's department cars and deputies blocking her way. Panic struck as she realized her mother was the reason. At about 10:30 p.m., Dorothy had taken Molly the parrot into the bathroom, locked the door, and shot herself in the chest with a .25-caliber pistol.[11] Allan heard the gunshot and rushed downstairs, but it was too late. Marlo, then eight years old, was in her bedroom asleep.

Bitter, frantic scenes occurred as Letisha tried to enter the house but was blocked by deputies.[12] Allan rushed out yelling abuse at the cops and had to be forcefully restrained. Later, Letisha complained to Bill Cryer that she had been "manhandled" by the deputies and that her mother "died because people tormented her. . . . People just couldn't leave her alone." Letisha was "tired of people treating my father like a dog," she said. "I love my dad. I'm not ashamed of him. Your parents are your best friends. Once your parents are dead, you have nothing."

No reporter could have handled the assignment with more sensitivity than Bill Cryer. The writing in "Dorothy Smith's Strong Will Finally Broke" quivers on the knife edge between objectivity and tearful heartbreak. You can almost see the empty box of Kleenex just outside the margin of the page.

"Once, a year ago, after she had berated the reporter about his news coverage of her husband, she invited him to have a cup of coffee with her at the courthouse coffee shop," wrote Cryer, referring to himself in third person. On that day the disgraced bondman's wife seemed to be in good spirits. More recently, she had called for Cryer at home and talked to his wife Cynthia, confiding that she feared for her life. "She said she had a gun and kept her doors locked." On the other hand, Cryer wrote, "She was confident that he would be acquitted, that they would win their lawsuit and he would get his bail bond license back. It never worked out that way, and her world simply fell apart."[13]

The additional indictments against Frank Smith, including the obstruction charge filed in federal court relating to the murder plot against John Calvin Bailey and the arson charge filed in district court, were not prosecuted. As of January 11, 1985, Smith had served almost eight years in maximum security confinement and accrued more than twelve and a half years of "good time credit." He was eligible for parole.[14] Ronnie Earle, just beginning his third term as district attorney, issued a statement: "We're opposed, strongly. He got a life sentence. He ought to serve it."

Smith served almost five more years before being released on parole to Williamson County in October 1990. Under the conditions of his parole, Smith was banned from entering either Travis or Gillespie Counties, except to see his doctor or lawyer. Earle was not overjoyed. "I am concerned," he said in a terse statement, "that he abide by the law and that includes the restrictions on where he lives."[15]

At age sixty-two, Frank did seem to exude less potential for threat, menace, and trickery than previously. His appearance had something to do with the impression. Thick, white muttonchops erupted, clownlike, from under his "Welcome Back Frank!" gimme cap. Along with his slow gait, he had difficulty breathing and showed other symptoms of advanced congestive heart failure. The prison bars were gone now, but his precarious health constituted yet another set of restraints on his freedom.

When *Statesman* reporter Linda Latham Welch came to visit, Frank prattled along about his brood of grandkids and how his cat had just given birth to six kittens. He maintained that he was just an old man on medication who had spent a third of his life in prison, and he wasn't blaming anyone for his problems—except when he claimed to be an innocent victim of a conspiracy, persecuted by "paranoid" cops and prosecutors.

"I don't know how a preacher's son ends up in prison three times," he said. "I guess I became disenchanted with the system and how crooked it was. I don't have no answer." For a person who had always seemed uniquely enchanted by crime and corruption, it was a remarkably reflexive piece of rhetoric.

He claimed that he owned nothing except for "a ten and a half carat diamond ring and a Rolex watch," leaving out a bit of real estate in Austin and a home in Hutto purchased by Abu Dhabi, the family trust.[16]

Letisha spent a lot of time with Frank after his release. "It was the closest I'd ever been with Dad," she said. "He had totally changed his life around. He found the Lord. He had become very religious."

The old, capricious, mischievous streak in him had not completely disappeared, however. Frank repeatedly violated his parole by venturing into Austin whenever it suited him. In December 1992 he was arrested while working at Frank Junior's auto parts store.[17] Another trip to Austin landed Frank in jail shortly after the new year. His friend, attorney Larry Dowling, represented him at the subsequent parole hearing in Georgetown. "They were trying to revoke his parole," he said. "Ronnie Earle came over to testify. We just had a hell of a hearing, and I won it."

On a subsequent trip to Austin, Frank made a conspicuous circuit through the courthouse. He even dropped by Travis County sheriff Terry Keel's office and left his business card with the receptionist. "It was more or less a message from Frank to me," said Keel, "that despite the fact that I arrested him for violating parole, that he was around."[18]

Then, on October 28, 1993, Frank Hughey Smith Sr. made his last appearance on the *Statesman*'s front page. There was his rascally grin, shaded by the bill of his "Welcome Back, Frank!" cap, and the headline, "Smith, an Ex-crime Boss and Bail Bondsman, Dies." The mighty oak had been felled by a massive heart attack. Letisha blamed the attack on her father's most recent jail stint and court hassles over his parole violations. Reporter David Matustik did a laudable job of threading the dead man's unusual biography through a remarkable collection of quotes from people who had known him. The result was the kind of obituary that one hopes to read when the subject is a legend, "a walking contradiction, partly truth and partly fiction" (apologies to Kris Kristofferson, who was singing about a very different type of seeker).

Attorney Larry Dowling said he had grown quite close to his client. "When he got out of jail he was on parole; he could only come into Travis County in order to talk to me because I was his attorney," he said. "And so Frank would come over and we'd drink whiskey and talk about the law, and we had many nights whiskey drinking and talking about the law." Dowling shared with me several astonishing Frank Smith anecdotes I had heard nowhere else. "Frank and I were really close," he said. "I still miss the guy."

The quotes Dowling gave Matustik, excerpted below, gave the piece a lyrical, almost mythical bent.

Frank had a lot of friends in high places as well as low places. He knew where all the bodies were buried. He took the whereabouts to the grave with him.

He was not a bully, but if you showed disrespect for his wife, you would get an ass kickin'.

He was a frontiersman. He hated authority of any kind. He hated the government. He hated police.

He loved children, old people, women, and funerals. He'd go 300 miles to go to a funeral of someone he barely knew. He felt like you became a better person by going to a funeral. It was just the Baptist in him, I suppose.

Doyne Bailey spoke for the many people who'd crossed paths with Smith years earlier and were left with strong but mixed feelings about the experience. "He had the potential for being a pleasant guy to be around," Bailey told Matusik. "He had this other side, though, that when he got a burr under his saddle blanket, he would stop at no end in causing people misery. In my short career, he caused more misery than anyone I ever dealt with."[19]

The reporter even collected a quote from Ike Rabb that sounded a note of empathy for his long-time tormentor. "One of the sad things about all this, he was a very capable and talented person—capable of a lot of good and what ended up a lot of evil," Rabb said.

Letisha Taylor wanted the public to know that her father had become a changed man over the past three years. "He said he wished he could do it over again and live a low-key life. What's important is what he was at the end." Later, Taylor added this: "He told me on his death bed he didn't do it, and the thing that bothered him the most was that he was running around on my mom all those years, but that's what the men did back then."

If Guy Henry Collins had any actual involvement in the plot to rob the Austin Salvage Pool, it was never explained to the public. He was never tried on the armed robbery charge. The last newspaper clipping I found on him was dated November 11, 1982. The 2nd Court of Appeals had just overturned his conviction and life sentence for possession of eighty-five tablets of hydromorphone.[20] He was forty-seven years old.

The old bootlegger Joseph Daniel "Red" Holt died as he lived, a player, just two years and two weeks after the ill-fated junkyard robbery. Nellie Callan, fifty-nine, of Choctaw, Oklahoma, told police that Holt had recently left his wife and moved in with her. Sunday morning, Red and Nellie called the police to report a burglary. The culprit was Red's wife, Roberta Holt, seventy-one. Roberta had entered Callan's house and taken away "items she considered hers": for example, a silver set and a television. Later, Roberta came back and threw rocks at the younger woman's house. Red came to the door to negotiate and she shot him. He was being taken into surgery when he died.[21]

Marnie Parker, who came to know Red Holt during the trial in Fredericksburg, vividly remembered the day she and her officemates in the DA's office learned of Red's demise. "This is going to sound awful, but I remember, we had a big chuckle when one of Red's wives had had enough and she did him in," she said. "News came out that he'd been killed by his wife and we weren't surprised at all."[22]

The Travis County case against Aymon Armstrong was not pursued, either, but like Collins, Armstrong and crime were never far apart. In 1978 the ex-hero ex-cop was given five years' probation after being convicted of a supermarket burglary. The burglars had almost gotten away with the safe holding over $11,000 by chaining it to the back of a getaway van and pulling it through a window. The van hit a pothole, the safe got stuck fast, and the whole heist went sideways. In 1982 Joe Lowe, a retired Irving police detective, spotted Armstrong wearing a ski mask, running away from a grocery store with a bag containing $40,300 of the supermarket's money. Lowe confronted Armstrong. Armstrong tried to shoot him, but his gun jammed. Lowe's 12-gauge did not.[23]

When the AP story about Armstrong's death ran in the *Statesman*, it began with the lead, "Aymon Roy Armstrong was a good cop and a bad criminal."[24] Unfortunately, Armstrong wasn't always a good cop. And when he was bad, he was really, really bad.

Among the many what-ifs inspired by this story, we might ask how the prosecution of Frank Smith might have turned out with a different district attorney in charge—former DA Bob O. Smith, for example, or Earle's rival, Ned Granger? Bob Smith had vast experience, but he was tied to the old courthouse crowd, where the good-old-boy ways of handling things were so ingrained that those involved had deluded themselves until the word "corruption" never even occurred to them: in that environment Frank Smith had been allowed to thrive. Granger was deeply involved in that miasma, too. By letting Frank Smith and other bondsmen slide instead of paying off their forfeited bonds, Granger illustrated how badly compromised he had become by those relationships, and the actions he committed during his last days in office showed not only his fealty to Frank Smith but also his low regard for the law and the people he had been elected to serve.

Ronnie Earle outflanked and outfought Frank Smith not only by using the immediate powers of the DA's office but by making a stand against the corrupt practices of the bail bond system and by rallying the powers of the grand jury, the FBI, and other law enforcement agencies. He stirred a sense of moral outrage against Frank Smith and his enablers in the Travis County Courthouse. Ned Granger was not up for the job, nor was Bob Smith.

The old-school crowd resented Ronnie Earle from the beginning and nursed their grudges long after Earle had proven himself. A lengthy article that ran in the *Statesman* in 1981 is so critical that one might assume they were reading acts one and two of a Greek tragedy, when in fact Earle had recently begun a second

Ronnie Earle, whose thirty-two-year tenure as Travis County district attorney earned him the nickname "District Eternity," here poses in front of one of his proudest achievements, the Children's Advocacy Center.

term, with six more terms and twenty-seven years to go. In many election years, he ran for reelection unopposed.[25]

Earle's first term was a time of shaking out, getting offices staffed and funded, and myriad other things, but it was not without significant achievements. In his first four years in office, he created two new specialty divisions, the Special Crimes Division and the Public Integrity Unit. The Special Crimes Division was created to investigate and prosecute organized crime, narcotics, and white-collar crime. The Public Integrity Unit investigated and prosecuted wrongdoing by state and county employees, elected county and state officials, members of the legislature, and others.

One of Earle's important early recruits for the Public Integrity Unit was Carol Fowler, the hard-nosed investigative reporter who had been fired from a newspaper in Amarillo for writing a bad review of John Wayne's *Alamo*—and who never looked back afterward. "Ronnie hired me out of the newspaper," she said. "He said he wanted me inside working with him instead of outside pissing on him. So I did most of the crooks who stole with their fountain pens. The Public Integrity people were mostly retired police officers, and they were always happy to go out and kick ass."

When the Public Integrity Unit turned its attention to high-profile Republicans, particularly, US senator Kay Bailey Hutchison and US representative Tom DeLay, Earle became the focus of bitter partisan attacks and negative publicity campaigns. Conservative media and politicians tried to paint Earle as a deranged hitman for liberal Democrats, calling him a "rogue prosecutor," "renegade," and "crackpot." The name-calling furor conveniently overlooked Earle's record: during his first twenty-eight years as DA, his office prosecuted fifteen public officials—twelve Democrats and three Republicans.

One of the high-profile cases was against state representative Gib Lewis of Fort Worth, a five-term Speaker of the House and one of the most powerful politicians in Texas.[26] A Travis County grand jury indicted Lewis for two counts of violating the Texas financial disclosure law. Lewis's attorneys howled that the charges were politically motivated; Lewis claimed that he had simply forgotten to disclose that he had solicited a $5,000 payment from a San Antonio law firm to pay part of a tax bill owed by Lewis's law firm. The San Antonio law firm specialized in collecting delinquent taxes.

Also forgotten was the Speaker's trip to a luxury resort near Acapulco, paid by the same San Antonio law firm. Lewis, four members of the San Antonio firm, and a lobbyist were accompanied on the vacation by six women, one of whom was a topless dancer. Another was Toni Barcellona, a twenty-four-year-old receptionist at the law firm. Lewis, married with grandchildren, had registered under a phony name and shared the most expensive suite at the resort with Barcellona. Apparently, the whole trip simply slipped Gib's mind.

Miraculously, the legal action by Ronnie Earle rattled the Speaker's attention so effectively that he made over a hundred corrections to his financial disclosure form. With eighteen months in jail and a $3,000 fine as an alternative, Lewis pleaded no contest to the charges, paid a $2,000 fine, and resigned from the legislature. The former Speaker left the Capitol in disgrace, and then, drawn like a moth to flame, returned as a lobbyist.

During the investigation Earle discovered an income report form in his desk that he had filled out but failed to mail before the deadline. The district attorney promptly fined himself $200 for the violation.

Travis County voters kept reelecting Ronnie Earle, and he kept seeking new ways of achieving justice for the community, not merely putting criminals in jail but finding ways to address the causes of crime, and of identifying and repairing the collateral damage caused by crime in the community. During his second and third terms in office, Earle began introducing programs that focused on community justice and restorative justice.

To address the harm caused by the vicious cycle of childhood abuse, Earle spearheaded the creation of a children's advocacy center, where abused children were interviewed in a child-friendly environment. Improved support for victims of child abuse led to more convictions of abusers. Earle also helped start the Child Fatality Review Team, supported SafePlace for battered women, and created the Family Justice Division of the district attorney's office. The DA's office also became home to the Family Development Center, which provided counseling, treatment, and corrections resources for family members who were victims of incest. The center was established by a committee chaired by Twila Earle.

The first victim/witness assistance division in Texas was another Ronnie Earle project. He was a "proactive advocate" for victims of crime, said Verna Lee Carr, director of the crime victims' advocacy group People Against Violent Crime (PAVC). "Ronnie's contribution and his legacy for victims' rights will forever be remembered. Nothing scared Ronnie. If he thought it was right, he would do it."

Carr was impressed by Earle's commitment to getting victims of crime engaged in the legal process. Because of Earle, she said, "a crime victims advocate now sits on the Board of Pardons and Paroles. Ronnie did that."

Earle was interested in the power of storytelling as a means for victims to piece their lives back together. "They come to see what happened to them in the larger context of their lives, and decide with a kind of iron determination that the perpetrator will not victimize them anymore," he said.[27]

In a speech delivered to a group celebrating the life of Nell Myers, the founder of PAVC, Earle said: "The law says that the primary duty of the prosecutor is to see that justice is done, but the law doesn't define justice. The question of what is justice arises in each case, and the answer does not lie in the law books. The answer is that the answer changes, because each case is different and has to be seen in the light of its own particular truth. That truth must be elicited from the stories of those involved. It is those stories that contain the raw material from which justice may be fashioned."[28]

Over the course of his eight terms as district attorney of Travis County, Ronnie Earle achieved or advocated for countless reforms in crime prevention, alternative sentencing, victim advocacy, and the reintegration of former offenders into society. Ronnie and Twila Earle both became nationally known for their advocacy of community justice and community building. They lectured across the country, together and separately. US attorney general Janet Reno was one of their biggest supporters.[29]

In late 2007 *Statesman* reporter Laylan Copelin called Ronnie Earle to ask the longtime DA what he considered to be the finest moment of his unprecedented eight terms in office. Ronnie was then sixty-five years old. The deadline to file for reelection was only a few months away, and he had not announced whether he would run again. As written, Copelin expected Earle to give pride of place to one of his scores of headline-grabbing cases against "murderers, serial rapists and crooked cops." The case against Congressman Tom DeLay for money laundering would have to be high on the list, if not at the top. Or one of Earle's many boundary-breaking firsts in the field of victims' rights, child advocacy, and crime prevention.

"Against all that, however," Copelin wrote, "Earle still rates his first big case, bringing down the late bail bondsman, Frank Smith, his finest moment."[30]

On December 12, 1977, Ronnie wrote a letter to Isaac Rabb on his office stationary. It began, "My Dear Isaac." He had been planning to write "for some time now" but the struggle to "put into words what we have endured together" held him back. Sitting on a hill with his dog, he had finally figured out how to say it. "How marvelous it must be to have a father like you," he wrote. "Not many men these days have the distinction of being clothed with honor before their children during their lifetime. I do not speak of your actions on December 3 alone; the courage I refer to is of a different kind. It began long before that Friday, and it ended when that beast was sent to prison. What happened on December 3 was courageous and amazing, but the memory I will always cherish of you, and that which I hope your children will remember, is of the man who for several years struggled daily in a battle for right.

"You should know that you have served as an inspiration to me," the letter continued. "You have thanked me many times. Please know that you don't need to. It is I who should thank you for giving me the opportunity to be part of a real, honest-to-God struggle against evil. It came at a good time for me, and it is a high point of my life."

Finally, Earle wrote, "Someday soon, when they get a little older, I would like for my children to meet you. Until then, let me know if I can help."

The letter was signed, "Yours very truly, Ronnie."

A postscript was added: "P.S. While this letter was being typed the delicious candy from you, Jane, and the children arrived. You and your family mean a great deal to all of us in this office and we appreciate your thoughtfulness. Thank you."

The letter expresses both the emotional and the intellectual sides of Ronnie Earle. The boy who grew up on a ranch near Birdville was a world apart, but only a stone's throw, from the Haltom City mean streets of Willie McKnight and Aymon Armstrong. Ronnie, who loved Zane Grey Westerns and wandering through the pastures as a youth, came down to Austin, where the sixties caught his imagination, and he devoted his heart and mind to law and justice.

All the mythic components for the struggle for justice on the frontier are present in this simple, heart-felt letter. It's *High Noon* on a junkyard stage. Dalton Lane is a raw frontier town. Ike Rabb and his family are earnest homesteaders, hoping to stake an outpost there, one foot in the rattlesnake wilderness and one in the nascent future. Frank Smith is the villain, and the sheriff is in cahoots. Ike Rabb, a simple man protecting his family and the spineless people of this town, is the only hope for survival until justice can catch up to this lawless frontier. Ike steps up to the challenge. He wins the short-term battle, but to survive and prosper, he needs the law on his side. There must be justice. That is where Ronnie Earle steps in. Frank Smith is brought to justice, and the town is saved.

For Earle, Western novels and the mythology of the American frontier were not simply escapist entertainment; he looked back on this historical period for inspiration for a more ideal society. In countless speeches over the years, Earle would insert the following:

There was a time when everyone was responsible for the community. Some rode out in the posse and confronted the offender and others stayed home and tended the watch fire and comforted the victims, but everybody was involved. Everybody had a stake.

In 2018 Ronnie and Twila Earle participated in the ribbon-cutting ceremony at the dedication of the new downtown DA's office, named in his honor, the Ronald Earle Building. Etched on a plaque inside is another of Earle's sayings:

> This building is where justice is to be done. That makes it a sacred place. Justice is the highest expression of the human spirit. It calls us to be better than we are. We may all hope that we honor that call.

Ronnie Earle died after a long illness on April 5, 2020. In one of her first conversations with the author, Twila said that if things had worked out differently, Ronnie would have been eager to participate in this book. His friends said that he enjoyed telling stories about the thugs and underworld characters of Austin, Fort Worth, and Dallas. Where those stories would have taken this narrative, we can only guess, but it undoubtedly would have made a rich and spicy bowl of Texas chili.

ACKNOWLEDGMENTS

The biggest thank you of all is owed to my wife, Lois Richwine, who, as always, kept taking superb care of us during the year I spent working on this little book, a year that coincidentally began with the Covid-19 pandemic shutdown of life as we had known it, and what I originally told her would be "a little book . . . a few months of work at the most . . ." (insert laugh track here).

Following pandemic protocols, all interviews during lockdown were conducted via phone, text message, email, and Facetime, except for a short, socially distanced Starbucks meeting with Bill Cryer. There were none of the usual trips to archives or anywhere else, but thankfully, the staff at the Austin History Center quickly adapted to the new normal and were able to provide me with biography files and photos. Archivist Madeline Moya deserves a big shout-out of appreciation for her invaluable assistance.

The exciting and inspiring story told in this book was a huge part of the lives of the amazing Rabb family. Ike and Jane Rabb, Denise Ormand, Geoff Rabb, Jonathan Rabb, and René Rabb lived this story and survived it. The many scrapbooks assembled by Jane were a priceless resource.

Sadly, Ronnie Earle, the hero of this book, passed away shortly after I began interviewing sources. I consider it a small miracle that his wife (and partner in many of his innovative efforts to achieve social justice and reform), Twila Hugley Earle, responded to my entreaties. If this book has any value whatsoever, a great deal of the credit is due to Twila's bounding intelligence, powers of insight and observation, and generosity.

Producing this book would not have been possible without the generous assistance of these individuals, nor would not have been much of a book at all without the help and input of Carol Fowler, Letisha Taylor, and Tressa Granger. Tressa Granger not only introduced me to Letisha Taylor, Frank Smith's daughter, but encouraged me to pursue the idea and helped introduce me to many valuable contacts.

Many other individuals helped inform and enliven the project. I wish I could have used more quotes and anecdotes of the people I interviewed, but UT Press wanted fifty thousand words, not a hundred thousand. My sources deserve to see their names highlighted in the book, and here they are: Doyne Bailey, Ave Bonar, Mike Carlson, Verna Lee Carr, Charles Craig, Bill Cryer, Larry Dowling, Twila Hugley Earle, Stephen B. Edwards, Carol Fowler, Arnold Garcia Jr., Tressa Granger, Guy Herman, Jerry S. Jordan, Phil Lerway, Ron Littlepage, Denise Ormand, Marnie Parker, Bob Perkins, Geoff Rabb, Isaac Rabb, Jan Reid, Mike Renfro, Dave Richards, Dottie Ross (Harding), Steve Russell, Bobby Earl Smith, Broadus Spivey, John Sutton, Leticia Smith Taylor, Jon Wisser, and last but certainly not least, Nick Kralj.

Unfortunately, photographers for the *Austin American-Statesman* who helped document the events of this story, day after day, year after year, were not credited for their work, but I can't go without thanking the ones who gave permission for the use of their photos in this book: Jay Godwin, Alan Pogue, Ava Bonar, and John Anderson.

Finally, a double-wide thank you to my writers' support group, the so-called Knuckleheads: Eddie Wilson, David Marion Wilkinson, Kip Stratton, the late Jan Reid, Joe Holley, Tom Zigal, Christopher Cook, and Ron Querry. Recognition must also be extended to my great friend and counselor on Homer and ancient Greek affairs, John Hubner.

A huge thank you to everyone at UT Press for helping bring this book to fruition, but particularly to Edward "Casey" Kittrell for his wise counsel, creative ideas, and steady hand; also to Lynne Ferguson, senior manuscript editor, and Leslie Tingle, the copyeditor who was so perfectly suited to this task. Finally, a big shout out to Gianna M. LaMorte, assistant director, who bought espresso one day, asked what projects I had in mind, and after hearing about this one, said it sounded real cool. That is what finally pulled the trigger on this picaresque mini-epic of narrative history.

NOTES

AUTHOR'S NOTE. A DEEP DIVE

1. Allen Turner, "Accused Murderer Escapes Austin Jail"; John Sutton and Dave Mayes, "Junkyard Suspects May Be in State Ring," both Feb. 5, 1977; and Allen Turner, "The Party's Over: Escapee Goes Back to Jail," Feb. 6, 1977, all in *Austin American-Statesman* (hereafter cited as *AAS*). Also see John Kelso, "Suspect Asks for Execution"; Bill Cryer, "Bondsman Reinstated; Surety Firm OK"; and "4 Policemen Scolded after Inmate's Escape," all in *AAS*, Feb. 9, 1977.

2. Bill Cryer, interview with the author. Bill Cryer graciously gave of his time in a series of at least eight substantial interviews by phone and electronic exchanges from March 2020 through July 2021, including two in-person meetings in September and October 2020 and countless follow-ups via electronic exchanges. Cryer also read the manuscript and offered corrections. Subsequent quotes and descriptions of people and events attributed to Cryer are taken from these interviews, unless otherwise noted.

INTRODUCTION. JUNKYARD OWNER SHOTGUNS ROBBER: WAS IT A SETUP?

1. Bill Cryer, "Former Policeman Arrested in Junkyard Shooting Death," *AAS*, Dec. 5, 1977.

2. Eddie Wilson, interview with the author, Jan. 2015. I interviewed Eddie Wilson numerous times during the course of our work on the book *Armadillo World Headquarters: A Memoir*, by Eddie Wilson and Jesse Sublett (Austin: TSSI Publishing, 2017). Subsequent quotes from Wilson are taken from these personal communications unless otherwise noted.

3. Margaret Moser, "Bright Lights, Inner City: When Austin's Eastside Music Scene Was Lit Up Like Broadway," *Austin Chronicle*, July 4, 2003, https://www.austinchronicle.com/music/2003-07-04/166659/.

4. A fatburg, or fatburger, is a mass of solidified fats and waste materials that clog wastewater systems and can be as large as a school bus or even a passenger plane. See Chiara Giordano, "Biggest Fatberg Ever Found in Northwest Lurking in Liverpool Sewer," *Independent*, Feb. 21, 2019, https://www.independent.co.uk/news/uk/home-news/fatberg-liverpool-sewer-oil-grease-wet-wipes-fat-united-utilities-biofuel-a8790361.html.

5. Laylan Copeland, "Earle Jousts with the Powerful, Dangerous," *AAS*, Nov. 18, 2007.

BAPTIST PREACHER'S SON

1. Display ad, "Frank Smith Says 'Thanks!,'" *AAS*, Feb. 9, 1976; "Frank Smith, Bail Bonds Businessman, *Austin Sun*, Mar. 25, 1977.

2. John Sutton, interview with the author, June 2020. Further quotes from John Sutton are taken from these personal communications unless otherwise noted.

3. Cryer, "Bondsman Reinstated."

4. Doyne Bailey, interview with the author. I conducted a phone interview with Doyne Bailey in April 2020, followed by an in-person conversation in July 2020 and email communications during the same period. Subsequent quotes from Bailey come from these personal communications unless otherwise noted.

5. Handbook of Texas Online, s.v. "Great Depression," by Ben H. Procter, revised by Brian Cervantez, accessed Oct. 21, 2020, https://www.tshaonline.org/handbook/entries/great-depression. Graph of the US unemployment rate 1930–1945, Social History for Every Classroom website, accessed Oct. 21, 2020, https://herb.ashp.cuny.edu/items/show/1510.

6. Letisha Taylor, interview with the author, 2020. All information attributed to Letisha Taylor regarding people and events in this book is drawn from a series of phone interviews and electronic communications between April 2020 and July 2021. The conversations originated with an introduction by Tressa Granger in April during a conference call between Granger, Taylor, and me. Several lengthy phone interviews were supplemented by often-voluminous text messages on no fewer than twenty-five different

dates. Subsequent quotes from Letisha Taylor are taken from these personal communications unless otherwise noted.

7. W. S. Foster, "Observations" (column), *Waco Citizen*, Feb. 4, 1977.

8. *Waco Tribune Herald*, Mar. 9, 1946.

9. "Mrs. R. L. Smith Dies in Hospital," *Waco News-Tribune*, Aug. 16, 1950.

10. "Frank Smith, 22, Charged in Theft," *Waco News-Tribune*, Mar. 31, 1951.

11. Ricky F. Dobbs, *Yellow Dogs and Democrats: Allan Shivers and Texas Two-Party Politics* (College Station: Texas A&M Press, 2005).

12. *The State of Texas v. Frank Smith*, 1977, 216th District Court of Gillespie County, Texas, Case No. 2446, pp. 1483–1487, 1502 (abbreviated as *TvFS* in later notes).

13. Nick Kralj, interview with the author, May 2020 and Sept. 2021.

14. Mitchel Roth, in his review of the book *Walking George: The Life of George John Beto and the Rise of the Modern Texas Prison System*, by David M. Horton and George R. Nielson, *Southwestern Historical Quarterly* 110.3 (Jan. 2007): 419–420.

15. Foster, "Observations," Feb. 23, 1956, and July 3, 1969.

16. Bill Cryer, "A Man with Power: Austin Outlaws and Elite Know Frank Smith," *AAS*, Dec. 26, 1976.

THE EAGLE SCOUT

1. Carol McMurtry Fowler, interview with the author conducted in May and June 2020. The interviews began with two substantial phone conversations in late May 2020; follow-up conversations and additional electronic communications took place primarily in June 2020. Subsequent quotes from Fowler are taken from these pernal communications unless otherwise noted.

2. See Carol McMurtry [Fowler], "Alamo Lacks Reason Why," *Amarillo Globe-Times*, Mar. 2, 1961.

3. Michael King and Jordan Smith, "District Eternity: Ronnie Earle on Ronnie Earle," *Austin Chronicle*, Apr. 11, 2008.

4. Twila Hugley Earle, interview with the author. Quotes by Twila Earle are drawn from a series of communications that began with our very brief introduction by phone in April 2020. More phone interviews and conversations began in earnest in late June through July 2020. Three follow-up interviews were conducted in November 2020 via phone, email, and text message. Subsequent quotes from Twila Earle are taken from these personal communications unless otherwise noted.

5. Handbook of Texas Online, s.v. "Parker, Cynthia Ann," by Margaret Schmidt Hacker, accessed Aug. 19, 2020, http://www.tshaonline .org/handbook/online/articles/fpa18.

6. Quotes from Jan Reid are from "Ronnie Earle," *Texas Monthly*, Feb. 2005, https://www.texasmonthly.com/politics/2-ronnie-earle/.

7. Handbook of Texas Online, s.v. "Birdville, TX," by Brian Hart, accessed Aug. 19, 2020, http://www.tshaonline.org/handbook/on line/articles/hrb34.

8. King and Smith, "District Eternity."

9. King and Smith, "District Eternity."

10. David C. Humphrey, *Austin: An Illustrated History* (Northridge, CA: Windsor, 1985).

TEXAS PACKAGE

1. Bill Cryer, "Dorothy Smith's Strong Will Finally Broke," *AAS*, June 5, 1978.

2. Tressa Granger, interview with the author. Tressa Granger introduced me to Letisha Smith Taylor and offered much encouragement while I was writing this book. I interviewed her numerous times by phone between March and December 2020, with followup conversations conducted by phone and electronic communication during 2020 and 2021. Her assistance was invaluable. Subsequent quotes from Tressa Granger are taken from these personal communications unless otherwise noted.

3. Dorothy Ross, interview with the author, Aug. 2009 and Apr. 2020. Subsequent quotes from Dorothy Ross are taken from these personal communications unless otherwise noted.

4. Dave Richards, interview with the author, Apr. 2020.

5. Tom Barry, "FBI Discloses: Six Arrested Here in Vehicles Case," *AAS*, Apr. 28, 1967.

6. Nat Henderson, "Car Trial Testimony Closes," *AAS*, Sept. 16, 1967.

7. Henderson, "Car Trial Testimony Closes."

8. Nat Henderson, "Arguments Over in Auto Case," *AAS*, Sept. 19, 1967.

9. "Waco Minister Succumbs," *AAS*, Feb. 1, 1969; "Pastor Smith Buried," *Waco Citizen*, Feb. 9, 1969.

THE BIG HASSLE

1. Isaac "Ike" Rabb, interview with the author. After an initial FaceTime call on June 16, 2020, that included all surviving members of

the Rabb family, Isaac Rabb spoke with me by phone in June and October 2020 and communicated by email in June, July, October, and November 2020. Subsequent quotes and descriptions attributed to Ike Rabb are derived from these communications unless otherwise indicated.

2. Ike Rabb, diary, 1969–1976, 1–9. The Rabb family generously supplied me with a copy of Ike's diary, along with scrapbooks that documented the Rabb family's experiences with Frank Smith between 1969–1978. Subsequent quotes from the diary are cited as "Rabb diary."

3. Ann Marie Wagnor White died May 5, 2020. She was survived by two sons, two stepdaughters, and two stepsons.

4. Denise Rabb Ormand, interview with the author. Denise Ormand was an invaluable go-between for my countless queries for various members of the Rabb family. Following our initial meeting in June 2020, we spoke on the phone and by email numerous times in June, July, October, and November 2020 and in January and February 2021. We also spoke briefly in person several times when she delivered research materials to my office. Subsequent quotes from Denise Rabb Ormand are taken from these personal communications unless otherwise noted.

5. Geoff Rabb, interview with the author. Geoff Rabb spoke with me at length by phone in July 2020. He also helped clarify various details about the Rabb family and the salvage business in several other brief phone conversations. Subsequent quotes and descriptions from Geoff Rabb are taken from these personal communications unless otherwise noted.

6. Rabb diary, 2.

7. Rabb diary, 2.

8. The account of the troubles in the paragraphs above is from Ike Rabb's diary.

THE BEST JOB HE EVER HAD

1. Handbook of Texas Online, s.v. "Connally, John Bowden, Jr.," by Walter H. Gray, accessed June 14, 2021, https://www.tshaonline.org/handbook/entries/connally-john-bowden-jr.

2. Dave Mayes, "Bail Reform Being Smothered by Jam of Bills," *AAS*, May 26, 1975.

3. Bobby Earl Smith, interview with the author, Apr. 2020. Subsequent quotes from Bobby Earl Smith are taken from these personal communications unless otherwise noted.

4. Carol Fowler, "Law School Idea: 3 Council Members Back Personal Bond Project," *AAS*, Jan. 3, 1968.
5. Anne-Marie Evans, "Space Problems Are Mounting in Travis County Courthouse," *AAS*, Sept. 27, 1970.
6. Mary M. Moody, "Mayor Comforted by Talk with Judge on Pot Comment"; and Don Fisher, "Comment by Earle Defended," both *AAS*, Nov. 24, 1971.
7. "Judge Leaving," *AAS*, Aug. 2, 1972; and "Earle Named Counsel for Judicial Council," *Fort Worth Star-Telegram*, Aug. 2, 1972.
8. King and Smith, "District Eternity," *Austin Chronicle*, Apr. 11, 2008; and "Ronald D. (Ronnie) Earle," in *Legislative Reference Library of Texas*, accessed Sept. 9, 2020, https://preview.tinyurl.com/y4bq 2jnj.
9. Jim Berry, "West Austin Democrats Endorse Doggett, Earle," *AAS*, June 22, 1973; "Doggett, Angly Awaiting Runoff," July 18, 1973; and "Earle Sworn In as Travis Salon," July 30, 1973.
10. Wikipedia, s.v. "Saturday Night Massacre," accessed Nov. 13, 2020, https://en.wikipedia.org/wiki/Saturday_Night_Massacre.
11. King and Smith, "District Eternity."
12. Handbook of Texas Online, s.v. "Constitutional Convention of 1974," by Mary Lucia Barras and Houston Daniel, accessed June 15, 2021, https://www.tshaonline.org/handbook/entries/constitutional -convention-of-1974.
13. Rick Fish, "Conservative Bids Lose Out Locally," AAS, Nov. 6, 1974.

THE TWO FRANKS

1. Kate Alexander, "'Hippie Mayor' Gave Voice to a New Generation," *AAS*, June 8, 2007.
2. AP, "Briscoe Attaches Signature to $9.7 Billion Spending Bill," *AAS*, June 17, 1963.
3. "Bail Bond Regulations Approved," Nov. 21, 1973; "Frank Gets Bail Bondsmen Titles Task," Mar. 6, 1974; John Sutton, "4 Get Licenses for Bail Bond," Apr. 3, 1974; and Cryer, "Frank Smith, a Man with Power," Dec. 26, 1976, all in *AAS*.
4. "Frank Being Sued over Bond Rule," *AAS*, Dec. 4, 1974.
5. Mike Cox, "High Court Says Collateral Not Required for Attorneys: Lawyers Bonds Rule Legal," *AAS*, Oct. 14, 1976.
6. Russ Million, "Frank Smith, Bail Bonds Businessman," *Texas Sun*, Mar. 25, 1975.
7. "The Honorable Tim Curry, Criminal District Attorney, Tarrant County, to John L. Hill, Attorney General of Texas," Nov. 5, 1974.

8. Robert S. Davis, *Bail Bond Handbook 2019* (Tyler: Texas Association of Counties, 2019), 103.

9. John Sutton and Arnold Garcia Jr., "Bondsman 'Still in Business' after Board Delays Decision," Mar. 14, 1975; Sutton and Garcia, "Bond Case Seen as Sour Grapes," Mar. 15, 1975; and John Sutton, "Order Allows Bondsman to Work Despite Vote," Mar. 20, 1975, all in *AAS*.

10. John Sutton, "Bondsman Smith Verdict 'Winner,'" *AAS*, May 22, 1975.

11. Broadus Spivey, interviews with the author, Oct. 2011 and Apr. 2020. Broadus Spivey and I collaborated on the book *Broke, Not Broken: Homer Maxey's Texas Bank War* and had numerous conversations about notable characters such as Frank Smith. I transcribed the notes from our conversation about Smith in 2011, knowing that the anecdotes would be useful to me someday. We discussed Smith again by phone in April 2020. Subsequent quotes from Broadus Spivey are taken from these personal communications unless otherwise noted.

12. Janie Paleschic, "Frank Smith: 'I Hold No Grudge,'" *Austin Citizen*, July 13, 1977.

13. "Bondsman Smith Is Resigned to Possibly Losing License," *AAS*, Mar. 8, 1975.

14. "Board Must Prove Case against Bondsman Smith," *AAS*, May 10, 1975.

15. Jon Wisser, interview with the author, June 2020. Wisser and I spoke by phone in a congenial and extremely informative conversation that covered a wide range of subjects and descriptions of events that contributed greatly to my understanding of the workings of the civil and criminal justice system in Travis County in the 1970s. Subsequent quotes from Jon Wisser are taken from these personal communications unless otherwise noted.

16. Ryan Autullo, "Travis Wants to Combine Prosecution Offices— Will Republicans Approve?," *AAS*, June 6, 2018, https://www.statesman.com/news/20180606/travis-wants-to-combine-prosecution-offices—will-republicans-approve.

17. Dick Stanley, "Cecil Ned Granger, 1934–02: Lawyer, Mentor Inspired Public Servants," July 12, 2002; Arnold Garcia Jr., "Ned Granger Lived His Life His Way, Whether You Liked It or Not," July 13, 2002, both in *AAS*.

18. Garcia, "Granger Lived His Life His Way."

THIS IS WAR

1. Rabb diary.
2. Bill Cryer, "Smith Swore 'Declaration of Full War,'" *AAS*, Sept. 21, 1977.
3. The adjuster in question was most likely Paul Brown, who testified in Frank Smith's trial.
4. Rabb diary, 9.

HE CAN ALWAYS GO STEP ON BUGS

1. Dave Mayes, "Earle Grabs Lead in DA Race; Win without Run-off Possible," *AAS*, May 2, 1976.
2. Larry BeSaw, "Earle Isn't an Average Texas DA," *AAS*, Sept. 13, 1981.
3. Dave Mayes, "Texas Bail System: 'Lockups for Paupers,'" May 26, 1975; and "Personal Bonds Can Work," May 27, 1975, both *AAS*.

A IS FOR ARSON

1. "Car Lot Fire Investigated," *AAS*, Oct. 19, 1976.
2. "Fire Damage," *AAS*, Sept. 16, 1968.
3. John Sutton, Dave Mayes, and Arnold Garcia Jr., "Bondsman Files Lawsuit to Collect on Insurance," *AAS*, July 11, 1975.
4. John Sutton and Arnold Garcia Jr., "Bond Case Seen as Sour Grapes," *AAS*, Mar. 20, 1975.
5. Allan Turner, "Arson Suspected in Explosion, Fire," Sept. 21, 1975; and "FBI to Join Investigation of Fire in Blacks' Home," Oct. 10, 1975, both in *AAS*.
6. Larry Dowling, interview with the author, June 2020. Subsequent quotes from Dowling are taken from these personal communications unless otherwise noted.

THE ROBBERY

1. *Frank Smith, d/b/a Frank Smith & Sons Auto Parts v. Isaac Rabb, Individually and d/b/a Austin Salvage Pool*, No. 254,138, filed in 126th District Court, Travis County. The author's copy of this petition and the separate petition filed by Rudolph Robinson were found in the Frank Smith files at Austin History Center.

2. *Rudolph Robinson, Petitioner, v. Isaac "Ike" Rabb*, June 6, Rabb, and Austin Salvage Pool, Respondents, No. 254,138, filed in 126th District Court, Travis County.

3. Bill Cryer, "Frank Smith Ousted from Car Lot," *AAS*, Dec. 14, 1976; Bill Cryer and Dave Mayes, "Junkyard Owner Rabb, Family Living in Fear," *AAS*, Dec. 15, 1976; and Carol Fowler, "Jury Seeks 'Gangland' Telephone Records," *Austin Citizen*, Dec. 15, 1976.

4. "The Salvage Yard Shoot Out: The Story Behind the Holdup," *Texas Sun*, Jan. 1977.

5. Bob Perkins, interview with the author, Apr. 2020. Subsequent quotes from Bob Perkins are taken from these personal communications unless otherwise noted.

6. Bill Cryer, "Junkyard Owner Shotguns Robber," *AAS*, Dec. 4. 1976.

7. "Headed for Gatesville: Tough-talking Youngster Can't Seem to Go Straight," Oct. 13, 1953; "Boy Headed for State School Gets a Reprieve," Oct. 14, 1953; "Smuggling Dope Laid to Fort Worth Pair," Jan. 28, 1967; "12-Year Term Given in Store Burglary," July 19, 1967; and "Ex-officer Arrested in Slaying Try," Dec. 5, 1976, all in *Fort Worth Star-Telegram*.

8. Bill Cryer, "Former Policeman Arrested in Junkyard Shooting Death," *AAS*, Dec. 5, 1976.

9. Bill Cryer, "Shootout Auto Trace Shows Links with Trio," *AAS*, Dec. 7, 1976.

10. "Smith Refuses to Lower Bond," *Austin Citizen*, Dec. 7, 1976.

11. "Decorated, Suspected: Ex-officer's Saga Leaves Much Hidden," *Fort Worth Star-Telegram*, May 21, 1978.

12. "Aymon R. Armstrong, Private Investigator, State Lic. #1683, wishes to announce the opening of his office, Armstrong Investigations, Summit Bldg. 1500 W. 5th, 338-0341," *Fort Worth Star-Telegram*, May 26, 1976; Bill Cryer and Dave Mayes, "One's in Jail, One's Out in Junkyard Shootout," *AAS*, Dec. 10, 1976.

13. Dave Mayes and Bill Cryer, "Robbery Alibi 'Won't Hold Up,'" *AAS*, Dec. 16, 1976.

14. Bill Cryer, "Stickup Suspect: It's All a Mistake," *AAS*, Dec. 11, 1976.

15. Cryer and Mayes, "One's in Jail."

16. "Burglary-Prostitution: Six Found Guilty in Complex Case," *Lubbock Avalanche-Journal*, June 26, 1968.

17. John Makeig, "Man 'Would've Killed' as Favor to Friend, Investigator Claimed," *Fort Worth Star-Telegram*, Oct. 24, 1979.

18. Bill Cryer and Dave Mayes, "Shootout Suspect Arranges Bail," *AAS*, Dec. 16, 1976.

19. Bill Cryer and Dave Mayes, "Rabb, Family Living in Fear," Dec. 15, 1976; and "One's in Jail," Dec. 10, 1976, both in *AAS*.

20. Dave Mayes and Bill Cryer, "Bail Bondsman Smith Quizzed in Robbery," *AAS*, Dec. 18, 1976.

POWER

1. Bill Cryer, "Smith Bought Frank's Car," *AAS*, Dec. 26, 1976.
2. Bill Cryer, "A Man With Power: Austin Outlaws and Elite Know Frank Smith," AAS, Dec. 26, 1976.

STAR TIME

1. Carol Fowler, "Reporters Tipped in Advance," *Austin Citizen*, Jan. 31, 1977.
2. Another new county official in 1977 was Ann Richards, the future Texas governor and stateswoman, elected county commissioner for Precinct 3, the first woman to serve on the commissioners' court.
3. Ronald Littlepage, "Cut-Rate Settlement Wipes Out Bond Debt," *Austin Citizen*, Jan. 4, 1977; "Outgoing Attorney Sues Junkyard," *AAS*, Jan. 4, 1977; Bill Cryer and Dave Mayes, "Granger Settled Bonds Cheaply," *AAS*, Jan. 5, 1977.
4. Ray Mariotti, "Ned Granger's Poor Legacy," *AAS*, Jan. 6, 1977.
5. Ron Littlepage, "Judge Pulls Back Forfeited Bonds," *Austin Citizen*, Jan. 5, 1977; "Tracing Events to Indictment," *AAS*, Jan. 27, 1977; Bill Cryer and John Sutton, "Bondsman Smith in Three-Way Pinch," *AAS*, Jan. 10, 1977.
6. John Sutton, Dave Mayes, and Bill Cryer, "No Breaks for Smith on $200,000," *AAS*, Jan. 6, 1977.
7. Ray Mariotti, "Curious Case Raises Questions," *AAS*, Jan. 19, 1977.
8. Bill Cryer, "Hays Sheriff Denies Links," *AAS*, Jan. 23, 1977.
9. A cancelled check from Smith to Smithey was entered into evidence in Smith's trial for armed robbery and habitual criminality in September 1977.
10. Bill Cryer, Dave Mayes, and John Sutton, "Frank Returns Suspect; Bailsmen Lose Licenses," Jan. 18, 1977; and "Frank Smith Indicted in Holdup," Jan. 27, 1977, both in *AAS*.
11. Bill Cryer, "Frank Called to Talk to Grand Jury," *AAS*, Jan. 20, 1977.
12. Cryer, Mayes, and Sutton, "Frank Smith Indicted in Holdup," *AAS*, Jan. 27, 1977.
13. Dave Mayes and Bill Cryer, "Grand Jurors Call Smith's Associates," *AAS*, Jan. 26, 1977.
14. Jesse Sublett, *1960s Austin Gangsters: Organized Crime Rocks the Capital* (Charleston, SC: History Press, 2015); Nat Henderson,

"Austin Underworld of the \'60s: Overton Gang Capers Recalled," *AAS*, Aug. 13, 1976; "Nelson Money Involved in Massage Parlor Deal," *AAS*, Feb. 25, 1977; and SortedByName.com, SCHNAUTZ, ALICER thru SCHNAUTZ, JASONR, accessed Dec. 9, 2020, https://sortedbyname.com/letter_s/s131525.html.

15. John Sutton and Dave Mayes, "Junkyard Suspects May Be in State Ring," *AAS*, Feb. 5, 1977.

16. Bill Cryer, "Another Conspiracy? Suspect Seeks Smith, Frank Statements," *AAS*, Jan. 22, 1977.

17. Dave Mayes, Bill Cryer, and John Sutton, "FBI to Join Hunt for Bondsman," *AAS*, Jan. 29, 1977.

18. Evan Moore, "Travis Bondsman Is Indicted in Holdup of Salvage Dealer," *Fort Worth Star-Telegram*, Jan. 28, 1977; Mayes, Cryer, and Sutton, "FBI to join Hunt," *AAS*, Jan. 29, 1977.

19. Bill Cryer, John Sutton, and Dave Mayes, "Smith Planned Surrender," *AAS*, Feb. 1, 1977.

20. Article I, Sec. 11-a, *Vernon's Ann. Tex. Const.*, accessed Sept. 15, 2021, https://libguides.law.ttu.edu/vernonstx.

21. The testimony quoted in this section is taken from *Austin Citizen* reporter Ron Littlepage's Habeas Corpus Hearing notes, dated Feb. 2, 1977, found in the Travis County Sheriff Department's Frank Smith file, now in the author's personal collection. Doyne Bailey inherited the department's file on Frank Smith when he took office and gave it to me in 2020.

22. *Fort Worth Star-Telegram*, Oct. 18, 1966; and "Bogus $100 Bills Trigger Warning," *Daily Oklahoman*, Nov. 30, 1967.

23. Littlepage, Habeas Corpus Hearing notes, Feb. 2, 1977, Frank Smith file, author's collection.

24. John Sutton, "Witness: Smith Planned Robbery to Cause 'Anguish,'" *AAS*, Feb. 3, 1977.

25. Littlepage, Habeas Corpus Hearing notes.

26. Littlepage, Habeas Corpus Hearing notes.

27. Ron Littlepage, "Special Report: The Full Shootout Story," *Austin Citizen*, Feb. 3, 1977.

28. Bill Cryer, "Smith Mastermind? Salvage Heist Badly Bungled," *AAS*, Feb. 6, 1977.

29. Dave Mayes, "Smith Indicted for Arson at Salvage Yard," *AAS*, Feb. 10, 1977.

30. Letter: Ronald Earle to The Honorable Raymond Frank, Sheriff, Feb. 4, 1977, in Frank Smith file, author's personal collection.

31. Memo: Officer Thompson to Capt. Falin, Feb. 11, 1977, in Frank Smith file, author's collection.

32. Ronald Littlepage, "'I Am Innocent,' Smith Contends," *Austin Citizen*, Feb. 14, 1977.
33. Cryer, "Salvage Heist Badly Bungled."
34. "Venue Hearing Today in Frank Smith Case," *AAS*, Mar. 22, 1977.
35. Ray Mariotti, "Executions Cruel On or Off TV," Jan. 8, 1977; and James Trotter, "You Win a Few, Lose a Few: Washington Philosophical about Critics," Jan. 21, 1977, both in *AAS*.
36. Letter, Frank Smith to Sheriff Frank, May 3, 1977; and Letter, Frank Smith to Craig Campbell, May 27, 1977, in Frank Smith file, author's collection.
37. Letter, Craig Campbell to Frank Smith, May 27, 1977, in Frank Smith file, author's collection.
38. Campbell to Smith, May 27, 1977, Frank Smith file, author's collection.

THE TRIAL

1. "Smith's Trial Moved," *AAS*, Aug. 19, 1977; Ron Littlepage, "Frank Smith Makes Bid for Freedom," *Austin Citizen*, Aug. 24, 1977.
2. Wikipedia, s.v. "National Register of Historic Places in Texas," accessed Jan. 16, 2021, https://en.wikipedia.org/wiki/National_Regi ster_of_Historic_Places_listings_in_Gillespie_County,_Texas.
3. Bill Cryer, "Jennifer Barton Vanishes in Street Life's Shadows," *AAS*, May 8, 1977.
4. This account of Frank Smith's solicitation of murder and Bill Cryer's meetings with R. G. Lopez was derived from interviews with Cryer and from his published accounts, "Smith Charged in Murder Plot" and "Jailed Smith Set Up 'Hit,'" *AAS*, Sept. 16, 1977.
5. "Private Eye Lopez Immortalized in Song," *AAS*, Nov. 14, 1985. One place to find the song "Corrido de R. G. Lopez" is on the album by Johnny Degollado y su Conjunto titled *Un Amor Diferente*, released in 2013.
6. Pete Szlagyi, "Willie's Manager Loses Papers, Cash," *AAS*, Apr. 8, 1982.
7. Janie Paleschic, "Charred Corpse Missing Witness?," *Austin Citizen*, July 13, 1977.
8. *US v. Frank Hughey Smith*, US District Court for the Western Division of Texas, Austin Division, Magistrate's Docket No. 7700106, filed Sept. 16, 1977.
9. Ron Littlepage, "Smith Trial Opens: Change of Venue Sought"; and "Lopez Gets Death Threat," both in *Austin Citizen*, Sept. 19, 1977. Reportedly, the call came in at one p.m.

10. When the author was a teenager in the late 1960s to early 1970s, he witnessed this shameful treatment on numerous occasions.

11. Littlepage, "Smith Trial Opens."

12. Bill Cryer, "Smith Trial Begins with Robbery Story," *AAS*, Sept. 20, 1977.

13. Indictment of Frank Smith, Cause No. 52,244, *Texas v. Frank Smith*, 147th Judicial District Court of Travis County, filed June 26, 1977.

14. Ron Littlepage, interview with the author, June 2020.

15. "Killeen Man Receives Lifetime Term in District Court Here Today," *Fredericksburg Standard*, Sept. 14, 1977.

16. Cryer, "Smith Trial Begins," *AAS*, Sept. 20, 1977.

17. "Murder Charges Dropped: DA's Office Not Ready for Examining Trial," *AAS*, Feb. 12, 1977.

18. Crispin James, "Man Acquitted of Rape Charge," *AAS*, Feb. 10, 1977.

19. John Kelso, "Suspect Asks for Execution: 'Living just one big drag,' Says Brummett," Feb. 9, 1977; "Role Denied in Two Murders," Apr. 14, 1977; "Brummett Assessed Life Term in Slaying," Apr. 22, 1977; and "Brummett Pleads Guilty," Apr. 28, 1977, all in *AAS*.

20. "Man Indicted for Murder: Cooney Slaying Suspect at Large," *AAS*, May 27, 1977.

21. Dave Mayes, "State Agency Exec Charged with Threat to Grand Juror," June 25, 1977; and Mayes, "Deal Offered in Insurance Investigation," June 29, 1977, both in *AAS*.

22. "D.A.'s Probe Yarbrough 'Death Plot,'" June 26, 1977; Jim Baker, "Yarbrough Ready to Fight Charges," Sept. 8, 1977, both in *AAS*.

23. "Smith Trial Costs County $15,000," *AAS*, Sept. 22, 1977; US Inflation Calculator, accessed June 24, 2021, https://www.usinflationcalculator.com/.

24. Stephen B. Edwards, interview with the author, June 2020. Subsequent quotes from Stephen Edwards are taken from this personal communication unless otherwise noted.

25. Bill Cryer, "Witness at Smith Trial Tells of Plan for Killing," *AAS*, Sept. 22, 1977.

26. Bill Cryer, "Defense Aims Guilt at Smith Pal," *AAS*, Sept. 23, 1977; Ron Littlepage, "Smith Defense Proves Surprise," *Austin Citizen*, Sept. 23, 1977.

27. Bill Cryer, "Schutz Says Desperation Spurs Smith Tactics," *AAS*, Sept. 25, 1977.

28. Bill Cryer, "Holt, McKnight Placed in Motel before Robbery," *AAS*, Sept. 24, 1977.

29. Ron Littlepage, "Key Witness Links Smith to Crime," *Austin Citizen*, Sept. 26, 1977; Bill Cryer, "Alleged Smith Target Says Deal Discussed," *AAS*, Sept. 26, 1977.

30. Joe J. Joseph's JJJ's Tavern at 525 East Sixth Street was the center of a good deal of vice during its twenty-nine-year existence. One door connected JJJ's with a triple-x theater; another led to a massage parlor/dope shooting gallery frequented by Bailey and other denizens of the historic "High Street" of Old Austin. Today, 525 East Sixth is the home of the comedy and magic cabaret Esther's Follies. Also see Bill Cryer, "Smith Said Robbery 'Messed Up,' Prosecution Witness Tells Court," *AAS*, Sept. 27, 1977.

31. "Writer Testifies in Smith trial," *AAS*, Sept. 28, 1977.

32. Nat Henderson, "Car Theft: 5 'Guilty' of Conspiracy," *AAS*, Sept. 21, 1967; Bill Cryer, "Smith Told Plans to Torch Business," *AAS*, Sept. 28, 1977; Ron Littlepage, "Surprise Witness Implicates Smith," *Austin Citizen*, Sept. 28, 1977.

33. "4 Austinites Sentenced on Firearms Charges," *AAS*, May 13, 1977.

34. Broadus Spivey, who retired in 2019 and passed away in 2021, practiced law for fifty-seven years and during that time mentored an estimated two hundred law clerks, a large number of whom were former UT football players. See "Broadus Autry Spivey," *AAS*, May 7, 2021.

35. These and the following quotations from the September 1977 trial of Frank Smith are from the trial transcript of record, *State of Texas v. Frank Smith*, No. 2446, 216th Judicial District Court of Gillespie County, Texas, at Vol. V: here, 1416–1425, 1426–1437, 1438–1442, 1537–1546. Further citations to the transcript will be given in parentheses in the text: (*TvFS*, followed by page numbers).

36. Wikipedia, s.v. "Childress, Texas," accessed Jan. 25, 2021, https://en.wikipedia.org/wiki/Childress,_Texas.

37. Although Frank Smith indulged in this particular use of tobacco, he was a confirmed nonsmoker, a trait he shared with Raymond Frank as well as Sam Johnson, who quit smoking after being diagnosed with lung cancer.

38. Frank Smith's testimony in this section is quoted from *TvFS*, 1582–1696.

39. Bill Cryer, "Smith Case to Go to Jury," *AAS*, Sept. 30, 1977.

40. Bill Cryer, "Jury Declares Smith Guilty; Ex-bondsman Gets Life Term," *AAS*, Oct. 1, 1977.

41. Cryer, "Smith Case to Go to Jury."

42. Cryer, "Jury Declares Smith Guilty."
43. Bill Cryer, "Frank Smith Chain of Events Finally Leads to Courtroom," *AAS*, Sept. 19, 1977.

AFTERMATH

1. "Prison-Jail Sentences Pronounced," *Fredericksburg Standard*, Nov. 28. 1977.
2. "Jail Medic Chief a Danger, Nurse Claims," May 7, 1977; "Jail Medical Story Due Grand Jury," May 12, 1977; "Jail Doctor Charges Probed," May 18, 1977; and "Discredited Doctor Back at Jail," July 2, 1977, all by Bill Cryer, *AAS*.
3. Ray Mariotti, "Bedside Gun Shows Junkyard Crime Scars," *AAS*, Oct. 30, 1977.
4. "Smith Requests Delay in Trial," Jan. 10, 1979; "Suit against Smith Settled for $3,000," Oct. 3, 1979, both in *AAS*.
5. Alicia Pounds, "Austin Salvage Pool Acquired by Public Company," *Austin Business Journal*, Oct. 18, 2001; "About IAA," accessed Feb. 2, 2021, https://www.iaai.com/Company.
6. Bill Cryer, "F. Smith: 'She's Entitled to a Life of Her Own,'" Oct. 5, 1977; and "County Seeks $121,000 from Smith in Bond Forfeitures," Dec. 2, 1977, both in *AAS*.
7. "Frank Smith's Wife Drops Divorce Case" and "Charges Dropped against Witness," Jan. 13, 1978; Bill Cryer, "Frank Smith Talks of Prison, Future Plans," May 11, 1978, all in *AAS*.
8. "F. Smith's Son Held in Theft," *AAS*, Oct. 29, 1977.
9. "Two Granted Separate Murder Trials," *AAS*, Sept. 2, 1978.
10. Bill Cryer, "Sheriff's Appearance in Court Sought," Sept. 1, 1978; Cryer, "Smith Talks of Prison," May 11, 1978; Candice Hughes, "Warden Fired for Not Pursuing Frame-up of Austin Inmate," June 8, 1984, all in *AAS*.
11. Cryer, "Dorothy Smith's Strong Will."
12. Bill Cryer, "Frank Smith's Daughter Cites Sheriff: Mistreatment of Family Alleged," *AAS*, Sept. 3, 1978.
13. Cryer, "Dorothy Smith's Strong Will."
14. Jim Phillips, "Ex-bail Bondsman Frank Smith Eligible for Parole," *AAS*, Jan. 11, 1985.
15. Linda Latham Welch, "Noted Austin Parolee Starts Post-pen Life," *AAS*, Mar. 7, 1991.
16. Welch, "Noted Austin Parolee."
17. David Matustik, "Smith, an Ex-Crime Boss and Bail Bondsman, Dies," *AAS*, Oct. 28, 1993.

18. David Matustik, "Smith Dies," *AAS*, Oct. 28, 1993.

19. Matustik, "Smith Dies."

20. "Pantego Man Wins Drug Case Appeal," *Fort Worth Star-Telegram*, Nov. 11, 1982.

21. "Cityan Shot Dead in Woman's Home; Spouse Booked," *Daily Oklahoman*, Feb. 26, 1979.

22. Marnie Parker, interview with the author, June 2020. Quotes from Marnie Parker are taken from this interview with the author unless otherwise noted.

23. John Makeig and Victor Dricks, "Ex-Officer's Saga Leaves Much Hidden," *Fort Worth Star-Telegram*, May 21, 1978; "Former Officer Dies on Wrong Side of Law," *AAS*, Nov. 29, 1982.

24. "Former Officer Dies on Wrong Side of Law," *AAS*, Nov. 29, 1982.

25. BeSaw, "Earle Isn't an Average Texas DA."

26. Robert Suro, "Powerful Texas Politician Indicted," *New York Times*, Dec. 29, 1990, https://timesmachine.nytimes.com/timesmachine /1990/12/29/605090.html?pageNumber=9; "Texas Speaker Indicted," *Tulsa World*, Dec. 31, 1990, https://tulsaworld.com /archive/texas-speaker-indicted/article_5e89b446-8f33-5934 -be43-8bc2e16911c1.html.

27. Ronald Earle, "Nell Myers Remembrance," speech delivered at Nell Myers tribute, Sept. 25, 2001.

28. Earle, "Nell Myers Remembrance."

29. "Obituary: Ronnie Earle," accessed Feb. 9, 2021, https://www.dig nitymemorial.com/obituaries/austin-tx/ronnie-earle-9114183.

30. Copelin, "Earle Jousts with the Powerful."

PHOTO CREDITS

INDEX